CONTENTS

THE GUY'S GUIDE TO

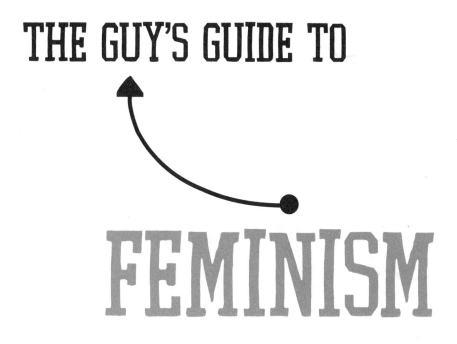

FEMINISM

MICHAEL KAUFMAN & MICHAEL KIMMEL

SEAL PRESS

THE GUY'S GUIDE TO FEMINISM

Copyright © 2011 by Michael Kaufman & Michael Kimmel

Published by
Seal Press
A Member of the Perseus Books Group
1700 Fourth Street
Berkeley, California

Library of Congress Cataloging-in-Publication Data

Kaufman, Michael, 1951-
   The guy's guide to feminism / Michael Kaufman and Michael Kimmel.
      p. cm.
   ISBN 978-1-58005-362-4
   1. Men--Humor. 2. Feminism--Humor. I. Kimmel, Michael S. II. Title.
   PN6231.M45K38 2011
   818'.5402--dc23

                                    2011019017

10 9 8 7 6 5 4 3 2 1

Cover design by Kate Basart
Interior design by Tabitha Lahr
Printed in the United States of America
Distributed by Publishers Group West

To the millions of feminist women around the world—and
the men who support them.

And to Amy and Betty, because the political is also personal.

• INTRODUCTION •

Both of us, both Michael K's, have had the same conversation over and over with the men we meet. Happens when we visit university campuses. Happens when we're speaking in a community. Damn, it happens with our own sons.

A guy stands up. Says, "I believe in equality and all that. But it's been years since women needed feminism." Another jumps in, "I mean, who actually calls themselves a feminist anymore?" A third says, "And even if they did, we've gone beyond all that women battling men thing, haven't we?"

We've each written a bunch of books and we each speak to a ton of men and women every year. But we figured it was high time that we actually answered those questions.

We believe that, whatever any of us think about the label, the ideas of feminism are still relevant.

More than that, we figure that these ideas are relevant not only to women, but very much to men.

And in a good way. One of the things we want to show is that in spite of all the garbage jokes and media stereotypes, feminism is also an amazing gift to us guys. Even if bits of it might make us uneasy, it holds out the promise of better relationships, better lives for the women we love, and better lives for ourselves.

Strange but true.

So, here it is, laid out from A to Z.

Read it. Cheer. Hiss. Laugh. Cry. Cheer again. . . . And then let us and others know what you think by visiting our site: www.GuysGuide ToFeminism.com; or Facebook page: www.GuysGuidetoFeminism/ Facebook.

• ALLY •

verb (ə-'lī, 'a-lī)

    1. to unite or form a connection
    2. to enter into an alliance

ALLY

Men as allies of women (men az 'a-līz əv wim'in)

    1. not an act of collective guilt, collective shame, or collective blame
    2. an act of collective love for the women in our lives
    3. strengthening our connection with women
    4. seeing that we have a common cause
    5. because we believe in the goodness of men
    6. what this book is all about

• ANGER •

A minister, a rabbi, and an imam were having a coffee.

The imam said, "This sounds like the beginning of a bad joke."

The minister said, "We're all the children of Abraham."

The rabbi said, "Yes, but which of his wives?"

The imam said, "Is that why feminists are so angry?"

The minister said, "What do you mean?"

The imam said, "They're angry at us for several millennia of bad things that men have done."

The minister said, "I like to tell my flock that women aren't angry. They're just insistent."

The rabbi said, "What's so wrong about a little anger? Imagine the world from their perspective."

At that moment another friend, a Buddhist monk, arrived. They told him what they were talking about. The monk said, "See the world from women's perspective? Well, let me start: How would you feel if every time you went out on a date, you worry you could join the one in four women who'd been sexually assaulted?"

The rabbi said, "Or what if there were people who wanted to make it illegal for you to have control over your own reproductive system?"

The imam said, "Or if you earned less for doing the same work as a man?"

The minister said, "If half the human race felt it was entitled to stare at your body or make comments about your breasts."

"And then, if you get angry, they accuse you of being a lesbian—"

"—as if that were a crime—"

"—or say how pretty you are when you're angry."

The four men thought about this for a moment.

"And it gets worse," said the minister. "Imagine that you start speaking out against these daily injustices and people start telling you to lighten up. Stop taking things so seriously. It's only a joke."

The rabbi said, "I wouldn't just be angry. I'd be ballistic."

It was Friday, and the imam soon went off to Friday prayers. "Anger," he said to the worshippers, "is a rational response to injustice. Anger can be a healthy emotion to feel, an expression that something is wrong."

The next morning at Sabbath services, the rabbi said, "Anger can be a motivating force, an impulse to get up off your heinie and do something, to at least say this inequality is not okay."

That afternoon, the monk said to those he had meditated with, "The problem isn't anger, it's finding appropriate ways to express it. Perhaps only by expressing it, can we ever let it go."

The next morning in his sermon, the minister told his congregants, "Anger can also be coupled with a desire to change things. It can carry a belief that things can change for the better. Resigned despair is what happens when you don't think you can change things. Anger can mean hope."

On Monday, the four men got together again for a coffee. They were joined by another friend, a Hindu priest.

The priest said, "But you're not saying that anger is the main thing that these feminists feel."

Now, this coffee shop had a waiter who'd been serving perfect cups of coffee for years. He'd heard the men talking the previous week and now heard this exchange. He'd often had this very discussion about women's anger with his girlfriend, so when the priest asked whether anger was the main thing feminists felt, he didn't hesitate to jump in.

"Excuse me," he said, "But when a woman feels angry, perhaps she is most angry that she has to feel anything but love and trust and how it feels to be an equal in the world."

The minister, rabbi, imam, monk, and priest nodded sagely to each other.

And that is no joke.

•AUTONOMY•

Imagine that you couldn't vote or couldn't go to college. Imagine that you couldn't work, or, when you did, you couldn't join unions or hold certain jobs. Imagine that you couldn't serve on juries or hold public office. Imagine that you were prohibited from driving a car, or from having a checkbook or a bank account with your own name on it.

Imagine that stereotypes about you were the basis for discrimination in employment, housing, and education. Imagine that you couldn't own property in your own name. Imagine that in the eyes of the law you *were* property.

Imagine that you were afraid to walk on the streets of your town or city, afraid to stay late at work or work late in the library, afraid to walk alone to your car in some parking lot. Imagine if you even felt afraid in your own home. Imagine that everywhere you turn, everywhere you look, your body is being used to sell things, from automobiles to stereo equipment.

This was the situation for women for most of the last two centuries. It was against this that women have been fighting. And boy, have they been successful—most of those rights have been won (except, alas, the ability to live without fear of violence).

Feminism is a political ideology that fights for the rights of women to be treated equally, without discrimination, and to make their own decisions about how they will lead their own lives. The idea of autonomy is the heart of feminism: "the radical idea that women are human beings," as one feminist writer put it. Autonomy means women can choose to become what they want to become, and to be safe in following their own path.

Is this really such a radical idea? We don't think so. It's nothing more than what men take for granted as our "inalienable right" every single day.

FEMINISM: AS AMERICAN AS APPLE PIE

If you think about it, women in the United States have been fighting for the same rights that were the basis of the American Revolution—the rights of individuals to find their own way, to make their own decisions, to live their own lives. The Founding Fathers fought for independence—of the colonies from Britain, and for individuals to make their own choices about their lives. They fought for autonomy.

Feminism in the United States was born of women's desire to experience the same sense of autonomy that the revolution had guaranteed to men.

We believe that men should support women's autonomy because we believe in the rights of individuals to make their own choices about their lives. We believe that men care about the women in our lives and we want—our wives, our mothers, our daughters, our sisters, our friends, our lovers, our colleagues, and our workmates—to be happy, safe, and fulfilled as human beings.

More than that, it will benefit us as men. It's more fulfilling and, frankly, more fun to be with people who are independent and strong, not supposedly weak, helpless, and dependent. It takes away some of the burden men often feel to always be in control, make the decisions, be the provider, and know where we're going without asking for directions.

•BEAUTY•

NEWS FLASH: Most Guys Dig Beautiful Women.

RESPONSE OF MOST MEN: Uh, you got a problem with that?

RESPONSE OF A LOT OF WOMEN: I feel fat. My boobs aren't big enough. Why's my hair so curly? So straight? Where can I get a pair of those pouty lips? Do these jeans make my butt look too big?

The majority of men are attracted to women. When it comes to heterosexuality, that's part of the deal. It's in our jeans and might even be in our genes.

The problem arises when a woman feels valued more for her looks than for her brains, personality, or skills. It's an issue when a girl is told by her teacher that she shouldn't worry about math: "You're pretty, you don't need it." It's an issue when women say that even in serious discussions at work or school some guys can't unglue their eyes from their breasts. It's a creepy problem when eight-year-old girls are pimped by advertisers to get all dolled up to look sexually alluring.

And it's a big issue that so many of the women we all know feel a desperate need to live up to virtually impossible definitions of beauty. Impossible, for one thing, because there's no timeless definition of women's beauty. What's considered beautiful changes from culture to culture, era to era, year to year. But relentless advertising hammers home only the latest version that applies to a tiny fraction of women. This has a terrible impact, particularly on girls and young women. Almost half of all *underweight* women think they are too fat. Over half of all girls are unhappy with their bodies by age thirteen; over three-fourths by age eighteen. Nearly half of all nine- to eleven-year-olds are on diets; by college, the percentage is over 90 percent. Who benefits? Check this out: The diet industry pulls in $33 billion per year worldwide; the cosmetics industry, another $20 billion.

Back when feminism first emerged, lots of guys thought women were overreacting to worries about beauty and advertising. But do you know what's happening now? Men are starting to get the same treatment: In our case, the main emphasis is how buff we're supposed to be. You end up feeling like crap if you can't land a job as a Calvin Klein underwear model.* No wonder increasing numbers of males work out obsessively, transplant hair, diet, or have plastic surgery. Psychologists call it "the Adonis Complex"—the constant measurement of our bodies against some Greek god–like standard.

So we can finally understand firsthand how oppressive it is to be pressured about how we're supposed to look and to be evaluated based on our looks. The Adonis Complex and the Beauty Myth: his and hers. This obsession for beauty can get under your skin.

Of course, this beauty question is a bit more complicated for straight men. We have to discover ways to allow ourselves to experience and express our attraction for women while at the same time challenging ways that we might degrade, embarrass, discomfort, or harass the women around us. One of the best ways to do this is to talk to women in your life about things you feel and the best way to express them. The goal isn't to become a sexless creature who can't delight in women and their bodies. It is to discover ways not to do so at women's expense.

---

* Author's note: For the record, both authors *are* Calvin Klein underwear models.

•BIRTH CONTROL•

But first, a word from the makers of Good Sex:

"Want better sex? Of course you do! Brother, does feminism have a deal for you. . . . "

Before we get slammed for false advertising, here's the thing: If you've got to worry that a moment of pleasure is going to lead to an unwanted pregnancy, it's going to cramp your style. For many generations, women learned to put the brakes on sex because they knew they'd be the ones to live with the consequences. Birth control is the miracle invention that frees women and men from this fear and opens the possibility for better sex.

That's right, sex just for fun.

(Of course, the other miracle invention that does this is same-sex sex, a.k.a. homosexuality, but here we're talking about the male-female thing.)

These days, most of us take birth control for granted. But that's only because feminists fought so hard for it since the beginning of the last century. Margaret Sanger, one of the pioneers of the birth control movement, was arrested for passing out a leaflet that told women how to limit births—as if mere knowledge of birth control was a threat to the status quo, which perhaps it was! Many other men and women (including Dr. Thomas Hepburn—actress Katharine's dad) have devoted themselves to helping women get access to safe, effective methods of birth control.

Access to accurate information and reliable birth control are the best combination for preventing unwanted pregnancies. We hear a lot of blather about abstinence programs—just say "no." Here's the thing. Saying no to sex doesn't even work as well as saying no to drugs:

In school districts where abstinence is taught rather than sexual responsibility (including birth control) there is now a higher rate of teen pregnancies and sexually transmitted diseases.

So why should we men support women's efforts to have access to birth control? Because it will enable women to plan their lives, allow women *and* men to decide when to have children, and give more people more options on what to do with their lives. Internationally, it is key for economic development and women's freedom.

Birth control is at least as much men's responsibility as it is women's responsibility. After all, what type of birth control is also the best method of reducing the risk for contracting HIV, the virus that causes AIDS? Condoms, of course. And condoms are a method of birth control for men. (Not us getting pregnant, but you know what we mean.)

Some men think they're not up to the task of being responsible for birth control. If we want to have great sex without fear of unwanted pregnancy or AIDS transmission, then we'd better take a quick lesson in sexual responsibility. Feminism has enough faith in men to know we're up to the task.

•BOOZE•

1. What was the focus of one of the early feminist campaigns?
   - a) Men's insistence on controlling the remote control.
   - b) Men leaving the toilet seat up.
   - c) Booze.

2. What is the most common date-rape drug?
   - a) Rohypnol.
   - b) Tickets to the Super Bowl or the Final Four.
   - c) Booze.

3. What is a common trigger for wife assault?
   - a) Beer.
   - b) Wine.
   - c) Hard liquor.
   - d) All of the above.

4. What can get you into a ton of trouble when mixed together?
   - a) Cement, bad debts, organized crime.
   - b) The name of your last girlfriend/boyfriend and the name of your current fling.
   - c) Booze, partying, sex.
   - d) All of the above.

THE GUY'S GUIDE TO FEMINISM

1. (c) Some early feminists were active in the Temperance Movement in the late 19th and early 20th centuries. The backbone of these movements to rid the world of The Evil That Is Alcohol tended to be conservative types. But some early feminists were aware of the relationships between drunkenness and violence against women and also how drinking destroyed household incomes. Meanwhile, of course, many other feminists fought to be allowed into bars alongside men. French feminists could never understand why anyone would want to stop drinking wine.

2. (c) Alcohol (sadly) is the winner. Although they may not be thinking about it as date rape, far too many guys will keep pouring the booze to get someone so bombed they don't know what they're doing. (See CONSENT.)

3. (d) Drunkenness doesn't cause wife assault in the way that beans cause farts. Booze is an enabler. It reduces a person's inhibitions and sense of right and wrong (part of what neuroscientists call "executive functioning of the brain"). And, for a guy who has a lot of pent-up feelings of hurt, sadness, and rage, this lowering of inhibitions can release a ton of feelings that get acted out in very inappropriate and destructive ways.

4. (d) See CONSENT.

•BRA BURNING•

Never happened. Well, not like they say it did. Yeah, there were a few bras tossed symbolically into a small fire in a trashcan at the Miss America Pageant in Atlantic City in 1968. But "bra burning" was mostly a media myth to ridicule feminists.

• CHIVALRY •

Is chivalry dead? Does feminism mean I can't hold a door open for a woman or pay for a date? Does it mean I can't compliment a woman when I think she looks nice?

Don't be ridiculous. Of course you can. Feminism is not a reaction against politeness or kindness; it's a reaction against inequality and the perception that women are weak, passive, and helpless.

If you feel kind and generous toward someone, it makes perfect sense to go out of your way for them. But ask yourself this: Are you doing it because you feel kind and generous toward that person, or because she's a woman and needs special treatment? Would you hold the door for a man?

So go ahead and hold those doors open—as long as you are not assuming that she can't do it for herself.

And go ahead and treat your date to dinner. Ask beforehand. A simple "I'm having a really nice time and I'd like to treat you to this dinner" would probably work. And then, let her treat you the next time. That way you'll have the pleasure of both giving and receiving that generosity. And that way, there'll be a next time.

•CONSENT•

Consent simply means "to agree with." It's a positive statement. And sexually, it's when both people agree about what's going to happen—and they let the other person know. There are four rules of sexual consent:

RULE 1:

When it comes to sex, only yes means yes. "Maybe" doesn't mean yes. And "no" never, ever means yes.

Unless you want to be committing date rape, you've got to hear a "yes" to have consent and, likewise, there has to be a "yes" on your side too.

Sample: "Hey, do you want to tear off our clothes and throw down like crazed weasels?"

"Yeah, that sounds cool."

That's consent.

RULE 2:

It's your responsibility to know if you have consent. If a cop pulls you over when you're speeding, it doesn't work to say you didn't realize there was a speed limit.

And remember, it's not her responsibility to say "no"; it's your responsibility to know she (or he) says "yes."

Some people say, "Well, how can you know for sure?" Our friend Harry responds, "Man, how could you not want to know? Can you imagine waking up some morning and wondering if you're a date rapist?"

RULE 3:

Nothing you've already done gives you permission to do the next thing. You're kissing like mad; she's totally into it; that must mean it's okay to get your hand under her shirt. Wrong. You've got your clothes off and you're all over each other; that must mean it's okay to have intercourse. Wrong.

The truth is that unless you're involved in a regular relationship and have already worked out a set of rules, every time you go to a new "level" you've got to get consent.

Some people say, "That sucks. That totally breaks the flow."

THOU SHALT NOT TRY
TO STEAL BASES

We'd be lying if we didn't say there's a bit of truth in that. On the other hand, by both knowing you're doing what you want, there'll be a thousand times more sexual energy than if one person is getting off and the other would prefer to be watching reruns on TV or is uncomfortable or scared. "Yes" is the hottest word in the English language.

Even better, because you'll know for sure and because both of you have to talk about what you like or don't like, we guys become much better in bed.

RULE 4:

If you're drunk out of your mind, you can't give or get consent. If either of you is too drunk or too stoned to completely know what you're doing, then it's impossible to have informed consent. You can't give it and you don't know if you've truly got it. Afterward, neither of you know if you're a date rapist.

If you're with someone and you make a decision together to get wasted and have sex, that's not assault because consent happened when you were sober. But, if it's the other way around, there can't be consent.

It's the law.

CUSTODY AND CHILD SUPPORT

It pisses us off when a guy doesn't support his own kids. I mean, sure, maybe he's sad or crushed at the end of his marriage. Or maybe he's happy to move on. Or maybe he didn't really want kids in the first place. Or maybe he's angry he didn't get custody and doesn't get to see his kids as much as he'd like.

Doesn't matter. It still pisses us off.

REASON 1: When he chose to have a child (perhaps by deciding to become a parent, perhaps by not taking precautions, or perhaps by getting together with a woman who has a kid), he's taken on a responsibility. Kids rely on adult support, and that responsibility doesn't have the same expiration date as a relationship.

REASON 2: His irresponsibility hurts his kid(s). Lots of children are hurt this way. In the United States alone, about 30 percent of all court-mandated child support payments are partially paid, and another 24 percent are not paid at all, resulting in nearly $13 billion a year that should have been there to help children.

REASON 3: His irresponsibility is hurting a woman.

REASON 4: His irresponsibility makes men look bad.

We know that when it comes to custody and child support, there are some complicated issues. Many of us know guys, including good dads, who've gotten the raw end of the deal in a custody case. We all know of guys who have had a sexist judge tell him he has to pay the bulk of child support even if his wife earns more than he does. We know there are judges who assume that a woman is the "natural" parent. (And let us tell you, most feminist women think this type of sexism against men is as bad as sexism against women.)

There are some groups that try to claim that men's anguish is somehow women's fault. They're called "men's rights" or "fathers' rights" groups. (Like Fathers 4 Justice.) They prey on men who've gone through tough times. They say that feminism is to blame and they play fast and loose with statistics. For example, they point out that women get custody in the majority of cases, but fail to mention that in most of those cases, the man wanted her to have custody. The truth is that most divorcing people get the custody arrangements they want.

One of the great changes is that *because* of feminism there are a lot more divorced women out there who don't depend on financial support from their ex-spouses, and who, without alimony, can fully share the costs of looking after their children. That's good for children and it's good for men.

Another great change caused by feminism is that these days most men *want* to share custody after a separation. You know, not long ago, many guys were more distant from their children. A lot of divorcing husbands wanted to "get away clean," free of family responsibilities.

It's pretty different now. Fathers are more likely to see their relationships with their children as the most rewarding of their lives—pre- and post-divorce. And to lose that connection is a terrible loss.

And the loss of that connection is felt by those very men who fail in their responsibility to provide child support. It turns out that these men have higher rates of death and suicide than men who do pay support. Thus, when a guy punishes his ex-wife by withholding child support, it's not only bad for his kids but it might also be bad for him.

And, frankly, that pisses us off as well.

•DADS•

Nowhere has feminism had a more wonderful impact on the lives of men than in our experience as parents. After all, feminism implores, encourages, and challenges men to be fully involved in parenting. It says we can do more than take our kids out for a special treat: We can be terrific parents.

Most men have stood up and listened. Most new fathers we know want to play a much bigger role in raising their children than did their own dads or granddads. Sure, some of the work truly sucks—but it's the best thing that's happened to men since the invention of the TV remote.

We still have our work cut out for us. In spite of these changes, women still do more child rearing in most families. This has limited their ability to pursue careers. It's also a total drag if both of you work outside the home and she's the one stuck with most of the work of looking after the kids.

And because children need all the attention they can possibly get, women also know that those children who do have fathers around will benefit from them being present and active, so long as these dads are loving and nurturing.

Scientists Solve Biological Mystery

(AP) Top scientists have finally solved one of the great mysteries of biology. In spite of many years when people thought otherwise, it turns out there are only two parenting jobs that men aren't particularly good at. Men just can't seem to get the hang of either childbearing or breastfeeding.

Aside from that, there isn't a single parenting activity that men can't do just as well as women. Asked to comment, Dr.

PAID FATHERS' LEAVE AROUND THE WORLD

NORWAY	80% of pay for 45 weeks, or 100% of pay for 35 weeks shared with the mother, plus 1 extra year of unpaid leave.
CANADA	55% of salary for 35 weeks (shared with mother)
AUSTRALIA	18 weeks at federal minimum wage
UNITED KINGDOM	2 weeks paid leave
PHILIPPINES	7 paid days
RWANDA	2 days
SAUDI ARABIA	1 day
US	0

More and more men are realizing that being a fully active coparent is something they want in their lives. We don't want to blindly follow a career that is "for our family" who we don't even know. That's why more of us have welcomed the responsibility to learn parenting skills and to arrange our lives to be active dads. Between 1997 and 2008, the number of hours every day that men spent with their children nearly doubled—from two to three hours. (Women's time remained constant at 3.8 hours a day.) And younger dads (with younger children) spend 4.3 hours a day with their children (their wives spend five hours a day). Men aren't just walking their talk; they seem to be jogging it.

It's also why more of us are supporting public policies that make ours a more child-friendly country, including publicly funded daycare and a better healthcare system. We can look with admiration to countries such as Sweden where programs allow either parent to work part-time or take a whole year off during the first six years of a child's life without any loss of seniority.

DOMESTIC VIOLENCE / WIFE ASSAULT

"How do I love thee? Let me count the ways...."

Well, there are slaps, punches, kicks, shoves, and threats. There are knives, guns, and sticks. There is severe emotional and psychological abuse. There is the taking of control over who she talks to, as well as totalitarian control over family finances.

Funny way to treat someone you love.

Most of us wouldn't dream of doing any of those things. Sadly, though, there are men (and some women) out there who don't share our dream.

MYTH: Wife assault isn't that big a problem.

FACT: We now have high quality surveys based on precise questions about violence. In the United States and Canada, reliable studies show that between 23 and 25 percent of women have experienced physical violence from a husband or boyfriend. A huge multicountry study conducted by the World Health Organization showed that around the world, levels range from 23 to 49 percent.

MYTH: Wife assault happens because some men can't manage their anger.

FACT: On one level, that's true. But it's a superficial explanation. After all, these men don't beat up people at work or on the street. Many are model citizens or the regular guy you know from school. Some men use violence like a tool: He uses it to control a woman, to have power over her. But, strangely, he also uses it because he feels he doesn't have power in his life so he uses violence to prove to himself and those around him that he is a real man. Some men use violence because they experienced violence as a child—against their mom or against themselves—and learned it is acceptable. And they use violence because, for too long, no one stopped them: Lawmakers, police, courts, and religious leaders turned a blind eye.

MYTH: *Women stay in abusive relationships because it's okay with them.*

FACT: Not a chance. Some stick around out of sheer terror (and, indeed, the most common time for a man to murder a woman is when she leaves him). Some stick around because they don't have any money (in some cases because the man didn't let the woman work or because he controlled the family finances), and they don't know how they will support themselves and their children. Some women may believe that if they love him more, or better, he'll stop. Some stick around because they see his good side or feel sorry for him or believe it when he says, yet again, that he won't hit her anymore. Some sacrifice themselves because they are afraid he will go after the children.

MYTH: *Women give as good as they get. There's as much violence by women against men as vice versa.*

FACT: No one says that women are pure and innocent. And we'd be the first to say that if a woman uses violence (not in self-defense) then it's just as wrong as if a man abuses a woman. But here are the facts: In good studies, we see that if you ask very broad questions about violence—Have you ever been pushed, hit, punched, etc., by an intimate partner?—then the numbers are roughly equal both ways. But if you ask whether the violence caused the person to go to a doctor, or miss work, or caused physical damage, then, overwhelmingly, there is much more violence by men against women. Furthermore, most men who do experience some form of violence in a relationship do not live in fear of this violence, but this is not true for many women. And a significant portion of women's violence is in self-defense or is a final outburst against years of abuse. Like we say, violence in a relationship is wrong no matter who does it (except, we would add, when it is in self-defense), but it's not equal going both ways.

• EDUCATION •

SCIENCE NEWS FLASH (1873)

Some startling research proves once and for all that it's a bad idea for women to be educated. Careful observation shows that women who go to college have fewer children. The reason, Harvard professor Edward Clarke tells us, is obvious: Allowing women's brains to grow means their wombs will shrink. The conclusion: Since this could lead to depopulation, it's best to keep women out of the classroom.

DEMOGRAPHY NEWS FLASH (2010s)

In our colleges and universities, well over 50 percent of students are women. They're the majority of medical students, law students, and business students.

WHAT HAPPENED IN BETWEEN?

Hypothesis One: In the 1880s, women's dresses were too large to fit into classroom seats. Styles have changed, so now women can get an education.
Hypothesis Two: Feminism.

DISCUSSION

We'd all agree that education is key for anyone to better him- or herself. The United Nations calls education a fundamental human right. It's key for anyone to really be able to participate in a democracy.

It's also key for societies to grapple with deep-seated problems, such as disease, unemployment, overpopulation, and inequality.

Although the number of women in higher education crept up progressively during the last century, it wasn't until the rise of feminism in the late 1960s that it really exploded.

That's because women realized the obvious: They were as capable as men in intellectual achievement. They had the right to pursue careers just like men. Meanwhile, the economy was changing and families required two income earners. And to seal the deal, the availability of birth control (fought for by feminists) meant that women could pursue an education without interruption by unwanted pregnancies.

More than that, feminists on campus figured that the lives and experiences of half the population was a subject worth studying. They wondered why women's experiences were secondary in history courses, why women scientists and writers were underrepresented in the curriculum. They figured this meant the usual curriculum was "men's studies." So they decided to create a whole new field called "women's studies."

OH YEAH

It's true. As that Harvard professor observed way back in 1873, when women get more education, they *do* have fewer babies.

It's not because their wombs shrink.

It's because their options grow.

• EMOTION •

SHE SAYS: "I want to know what you're feeling."
He says: "I don't know. Tell me what I should feel and I'll try to feel it."

From day one, we're taught that real men don't show their feelings. Showing your feelings makes you weaker. Suck it up. Don't cry. Play through pain. Otherwise, we'll lose our stoic manliness and our ability to remain cool and dispassionate in a crisis. That winning poker face will disappear forever.

Sometimes we think that being a man and being reliable in a crisis means being an inanimate object—a rock, a pillar, a "sturdy oak."

But does it really? Who would you rather interact with when you're in a crisis: someone who shows no emotion at all, or someone who recognizes the seriousness of the crisis? We're not talking about someone who gets hysterical and out of control here; that's no good for a woman or a man. We're talking about responsiveness.

Expressing emotions is a vital part of being human. Keeping them inside is bad politics and bad for our health.

Of course, men do feel we have permission to express one emotion. Anger. Whether it's road rage on the freeway, or vitriolic hatred of your political enemies, or the venomous taunting of other teams, or vengeful animosity toward a girlfriend who just dumped you, anger is the one feeling we can have.

But that is not the only emotion, nor even the only one that we express. Ever listen to country musicians wail in anguish over a breakup? Or watch athletes cry after a bitter loss? Or soldiers weep at the death of a comrade? Or watch men celebrate any sort of triumph? Or watch a man witnessing the birth of his baby?

The truth is, we feel and express emotions all the time. But we've inherited an idea of masculinity that seems to depend on their suppression.

Sometimes it feels that we have to unlearn the lie that the inability to express emotion is what makes us manly. What makes us manly is our *ability* to respond appropriately to a situation, to acknowledge our feelings, and to express them in appropriate ways.

EQUALITY, EQUITY, AND LIBERATION

Three key terms for your equality-minded-man cheat sheet:

Women's **equality** (or gender equality) means that women and girls have the same opportunities as men and boys. They get paid the same. They don't face invisible barriers that hold them back in the workforce. They're equally represented in government bodies, trade union leaderships, corporate boardrooms, etc.

It gets more interesting. Equality doesn't mean we're all the same. It doesn't even mean treating different people the same. That's where "equity" comes in.

Equity means fairness. So, for example, a nursing mother wants to be able to get back to her paid work. And let's say there is a childcare center at her workplace. It's fair that she be allowed to go nurse her baby as needed even though men don't get equal treatment—that is, the men she's working with may not have a break every two hours. Not equal, but fair.

Liberation goes beyond mere equality between women and men. The phrase that was used to describe feminism in the late 1960s and early 1970s was "women's liberation." The idea was that women didn't only want equality with men. As Timothy Leary once said, "Women who seek to be equal with men lack ambition." Feminism isn't only about equality. It's about the transformation of our ideas of gender and

ERA (EQUAL RIGHTS AMENDMENT)

A Modest Proposal (About Equality in the United States)

Ask people if they agree with this statement: "Equality of rights under the law shall not be denied or abridged by the United States or by any state on account of sex."

Hard to argue against, isn't it? I mean, who would say they *favor* discrimination?

This amendment to the U.S. Constitution was proposed in 1923 by feminist leader Alice Paul. She assumed that after gaining the right to vote, women needed an additional federal law that protected them from discrimination.

It passed Congress in 1972. But to become part of the Constitution, it required 38 states to agree. Only 35 did so.

And there it has languished. Reintroduced every year in Congress, this modest proposition is still not part of the Constitution—the document that says: This is how we think of ourselves as a nation.

freeing both females and males from the narrow straitjackets of what it supposedly means to be women and men.

Three key terms for your equality-minded-man cheat sheet:

There you have it:

Equality = Equal treatment, opportunities, and results.

Equity = Fairness.

Liberation = Transformation and true freedom.

Strong, equal, empowered women = Much better lives for men.

• "FEMINAZI" •

This term, popularized by right-wing pundit Rush Limbaugh, is a good example of the ways in which the backlash against feminism works. It consists of linking something you don't support with something that *nobody* supports, thereby hoping to win people over to your side. This is the trendy way to preserve privilege and resist equality in the guise of preserving equality and resisting special privilege.

To illustrate, take this little quiz:

A GUY'S GUIDE – TRUE OR FALSE QUIZ

1. Nazism was a political philosophy that involved totalitarian politics, the denial of rights, and a systematic plan for the genocide of several different populations (Jews, gays, gypsies, and Slavs).
❏ **TRUE** ❏ **FALSE**

2. Feminism is a political philosophy that involves the democratic expansion of individual rights, and a plea to end the violence and terror that is committed daily against women.
❏ **TRUE** ❏ **FALSE**

3. Rush Limbaugh believes that gays and women have too many rights, that Jews already control the world, and that America is too crowded with immigrants who should be deported and criminals who should be killed. Gloria Steinem reminds us that "Hitler came to power against the strong feminist movement in Germany, padlocked the family planning clinics, and declared abortion a crime against the state—all views that more closely resemble Rush Limbaugh's."
❏ **TRUE** ❏ **FALSE**

ANSWERS!

ANSWER SHEET

1. TRUE
2. TRUE
3. TRUE

Okay. Here's the big bonus extra credit question: Which philosophy is closer to Nazism, no. 2 or no. 3? Time's up, Rush.

• FEMINISM •

Do you believe that women should:

❏ Have the right to vote?

❏ Go to college?

❏ Drive a car?

❏ Open a bank account in her own name?

❏ Enjoy sex?

❏ Work in whatever occupation they might choose, and get paid the same as men when they do the same work?

Did you answer yes?

Then you better lie down. . . . You've probably caught feminism.

The feminist contagion has spread far and wide. It infects both women and men. Most people in North America, Europe, and many parts of the rest of the world have caught it. The terrible truth is that, nowadays, most of us support these rights and actually see them as basic rights of individuals in a democracy.

QUESTIONS FOR CONCERNED INDIVIDUALS!

What was it like before we had to worry about being infected?

For one thing, women had none of these rights. Ask your mother or grandmother: As recently as the 1960s, she had to get her hubby's signature to open a bank account.

How did the contagion spread?

Not by being ladylike. Women spent a hundred years campaigning for the right to vote (and winning it first in New Zealand). They fought for a century to control their own bodies and work alongside men in the jobs of their choice.

Yeah, but aren't things equal now?

This disease is relentless. Give 'em the right to vote and they want the right to equal pay. Give 'em that and they want childcare as part of the public education system. And, who knows, when they get that, they're going to expect an end to rape and partner assault. This disease knows no bounds!

Those infected will admit that things are pretty good here compared with some other parts of the world (and compared to even twenty-five years ago). But then they'll have the nerve to point out that even the United States has never ratified the United Nations' Convention on the Elimination of All Forms of Discrimination against Women; they'll tell you that Congress turned down an amendment to prohibit discrimination against women.

What are the two main symptoms?

The symptoms are simple and terrifying. It starts as one empirical observation (about the state of things), quickly followed by a moral position (about how things should be, based on that empirical observation). That's all it takes!

Here's what to watch out for: The empirical observation is that, in our society, women and men are still not equal. (Beware if you find yourself noticing men form the big majority of those who run local, state, and federal governments; major corporations; colleges and universities; religious institutions; and media conglomerates. Beware if you find yourself losing sleep because women earn about 81 cents for every buck that men make.)

The moral position is even simpler: It should not be this way.

A CONTAGION THAT SPREADS *EVERYWHERE!*

Feminism can spread into every nook and cranny. We're not just talking about public life, or jobs, or pay. Once the virus invades a person, it starts a mutation in their personal life! You start thinking that in our personal relationships women deserve to have total respect and dignity! That they should be a partner in all decision-making!

DOES THIS VIRUS TARGET MEN?

The virus really has it in for men. It doesn't believe that male biology causes men to rape or pillage or not listen. It actually believes that men are basically good!!!! That men can (and should) be ethical, emotionally present, and accountable to our values in our interactions with women—as well as with other men.

Women who've caught feminism not only expect men to act in honorable ways, but also have a deep belief in our ability to do so.

Beware, my friend. This is very insidious stuff.

WHAT CAN A CONCERNED GUY DO TO STAY VIRUS FREE?

❏ Watch out if you buy a T-shirt with a slogan like: "A Man of Quality Isn't Threatened by Women's Equality."

❏ Be scared, be very scared if you find yourself thinking that our masculinity is actually confirmed by our willingness to stand up for what's right, even when the cause seems unpopular.

❏ Run for the hills if you wear a T-shirt that reads, "Real Men Support Feminism."

FRIENDSHIP

SALLY: We are just going to be friends, okay?

Harry: Friends! Yeah, it's the best thing. [pause] You realize, of course, that we could never be friends. . . . Men and women can't be friends because the sex part always gets in the way.

Sally: That's not true. . . .

Harry: No man can be friends with a woman he finds attractive. He always wants to have sex with her.

Sally: So you're saying that a man can be friends with a woman he finds unattractive.

Harry: No, you pretty much want to nail them too.

That scene from the iconic 1980s movie *When Harry Met Sally* pretty much summed up the situation for decades. In fact, a lot of smart people figured that men were so emotionally shut down that deep friendships with either sex were just about impossible. (One psychologist even coined a clinical term for men's incapacity for emotional expressiveness: *alexithymia*. But don't worry, that's not on the final exam.)

Truth is, Harry was wrong. Men and women can be friends. Men and women are friends. Sex doesn't always get in the way. And even if it does, you deal with it.

But here's the amazing thing about friendship: You make friends with people you consider your equals. You consider your friends your peers. You don't make friends with your boss, or your college dean, or with some low-life you wouldn't want to be seen with.

What does friendship have to do with feminism, you ask? That's easy. Feminism encouraged women to be more assertive and confident. And feminist women encouraged men to be more emotionally available and expressive. And the more confident women get, and the more expressive men get—well, the more equal women and men are. And the more capable they are of being real friends.

Greater gender equality makes our friendships possible, which is great for both women and men.

Harry may have misinformed Sally that men and women were from different planets, perhaps Mars and Venus. Happily, we live on planet Earth—and we Earthlings are capable of friendships between equals.

• FUNDAMENTALISM •

Dear Dr. Laura:

Thank you for doing so much to educate people regarding God's Law. I try to share that knowledge with as many people as I can. When someone tries to defend the homosexual lifestyle, for example, I simply remind them that Leviticus 18:22 clearly states it to be an abomination. End of debate.

I do need some advice from you, however, regarding some of the other specific laws and how to follow them:

When I burn a bull on the altar as a sacrifice, I know it creates a pleasing odor for the Lord—Lev. 1:9. The problem is my neighbors. They claim the odor is not pleasing to them. Should I smite them?

I would like to sell my daughter into slavery, as sanctioned in Exodus 21:7. In this day and age, what do you think would be a fair price for her?

I have a neighbor who insists on working on the Sabbath. Exodus 35:2 clearly states he should be put to death. Am I morally obligated to kill him myself?

Lev. 21:20 states that I may not approach the altar of God if I have a defect in my sight. I have to admit that I wear reading *glasses. Does my vision have to be 20/20, or is there some wiggle room here?*

Most of my male friends get their hair trimmed, including the hair around their temples, even though this is expressly forbidden by Lev. 19:27. How should they die?

Thank you again for reminding us that God's word is eternal and unchanging.

Your devoted fan,
[Author unknown]

FUNDAMENTALISM, whether of the Christian, Jewish, Muslim, or Hindu variety, is a socially conservative political ideology dressed up in religious language. Although fundamentalists claim to adhere to the original doctrinal texts, they are frequently very selective in their use of those texts and traditions. (Check out the letter to neo-fundamentalist Dr. Laura, for example.)

As a religious doctrine, fundamentalism often takes religion out of the social context in which it first arose and says that tenets that may have made sense in, for example, a society that still practiced slavery, are still applicable today.

The societies in which all the world's great religions evolved were male dominated. It stands to reason that the original religious doctrines reflect the beliefs of those societies.

Someone who believes in gender equality and fairness may or may not be religious. They may or may not believe in God.

But when it comes to fundamentalism, it's pretty hard to fully reconcile the two because fundamentalists say that nothing should change from a few thousand years ago (although they only apply this to some things and not others).

It's no surprise that religious fundamentalism has emerged so strongly in the last few decades as we've achieved ever-greater equality between women and men. It is, in part, a reaction to the progress women have made. It's almost as if the stronger women have become, the more some people retreat to selected texts that say women are actually quite weak.

• GENDER VS. SEX •

"Sex" (in the boring form) refers to whatever might be the essential biology of males versus females.

"Gender," in the important sense developed by feminists, refers to our ideas of femininity and masculinity. It has to do with the relations of power between and within the sexes. It is the result of how we raise boys and girls to be men and women.

"Female" and "male" refer to sex.

"Men" and "women," "masculine" and "feminine" refer to gender.

Of course, it isn't so simple. For more, see XX/XY.

•GENITAL CUTTING•

It's something done to girls before puberty. Lots of girls. Two million of them each year. Amnesty International estimates that a staggering 135 million women have suffered this fate.

It is genital cutting. Some people also call it female genital mutilation (FGM).

The forms of this cutting range from merely awful to absolutely horrific: from slicing off the clitoris and part or all of the labia (the lips of the vulva) all the way to also sewing up the vaginal opening to just allow a small hole for pee to come out. (In the latter, women then get cut back open before their marriage.)

It seems that some societies so vilified women's bodies that both women and men got convinced that girls should have their genitals "transformed." It's still done to this day across sub-Saharan Africa, with some of the highest rates in Egypt, Sudan, Somalia, Ethiopia, and Mali. It exists in parts of Iraq, Iran, Saudi Arabia, and other Middle Eastern countries. In some places it's seen as a Muslim tradition; in a few others as a Christian one; in others simply as part of tribal cultures. Even in some industrial societies, there are women who have their genitals surgically reshaped and resized to conform to some notion of feminity.

Traditionally the procedure was done by women, such as a village midwife. These days, it's also done by big-city doctors who seem to have missed the lesson on the Hippocratic Oath where they pledge to do no harm.

Regardless of the rationale, this is a good example of women buying into some very nasty ideas in some male-dominated societies. And it's women who often make sure this is done to their daughters and it's been women doing the cutting.

Aside from the pain and trauma of the cutting, the medical consequences are huge, including serious illness or death from infection or bleeding, especially when it's done in nonsterile conditions. It can lead to very painful sexual intercourse and ongoing urinary tract infections. It can lead to terrible consequences while giving birth. And it can also lead to a huge loss of sexual pleasure.

The good news is that through the work of women's organizations, the United Nations, and a growing number of governments and religious authorities, rates of genital cutting are beginning to go down. In many countries, men have joined women in taking leadership to end all forms of genital cutting. For example, an increasing number of imams and scholars have signed fatwas (religious edicts) banning the practice.

•GIRLS GONE WILD•

"**I** don't get it," said Jack.

"What's that?" responded Jill.

"When my buddies and I get shit-faced drunk, you say we're immature and acting like jerks."

"You are and you do."

"And when we guys are hustling girls, trying everything we can think of to get laid, you talk like we're almost date rapists."

"Well, you do seem like a pack of animals."

"And if any of us get into a fight, you say that it's really screwed up how we learn to behave."

"Right again," said Jill.

"There's a big double standard going down here. I mean you're doing the same things as us these days. You drink us under the table. You're as raunchy as we are. You talk about men's bodies like we're pieces of meat. Violence by girls is on the rise. And you say 'Respect me for my brains,' yet you're on shows like *Girls Gone Wild* and *Spring Break* where you're pulling off your tops and showing your boobs."

Jill says, "I'm going to fetch a pail of water."

THE GOOD DOCTORS MK² weigh in:

Too true. Women are definitely capable of acting like jerks.

Then again, it's a pretty confusing time to be a woman or a man.

Lots of guys are challenging useless, old ideas of manhood. And yet, there can still be pressure to "act like a man" and we still meet women who are attracted to the old type of guys.

For women, it also can be pretty confusing. Women have redefined what it means to be a woman. Women know they can be assertive. A whole generation of girls has grown up defining themselves as strong and powerful. Feminism makes it clear that no matter how a woman chooses to dress, she's not asking to be harassed or assaulted.

Those are good changes.

However, we still live in a society that puts undue emphasis on how women look. That can't help but affect you when you're growing up.

And, sure, girls grow up knowing they're powerful. The problem is that the dominant way we define "power" is what you can think of as a "masculinist" way. To be powerful is to have control—over others, over the world, over your own body and emotions. And how do you achieve this control over others? Whatever it takes, including undue aggression and violence. This has been awful for generations of guys.

Sadly, too many young women are taking all this into their developing idea of what it means to be a woman.

It sets the bar kinda low, don't you think, to say that women's liberation means women's ability to make as big a fool of themselves as some guys do? Or to see their "empowerment" as the ability to objectify themselves before men get the chance? That's not the sort of "power" most feminists had in mind.

Feminism celebrates women as sexual beings. It celebrates women's sexual autonomy. These are great things. But we're living in a time of transformation about what exactly that might look like.

Jack and Jill
It's up to you
To stop worrying about that damn pail of water
And keep redefining what it means to be women and men and
to make sure that our behavior, whether in a bar or an office,
a bedroom, or a classroom, is respectful—both respectful to
others and, also, deeply respectful to ourselves.

GOOD RELATIONSHIPS: A RECIPE

This recipe generally feeds two people. (Experiment with larger numbers at your own risk.) It works whether you have committed to a lifetime of eating together or you have hooked up just for a one-night snack. (Modify the intensity based on length of meal.)

Blend together, the ingredients for respect:
- ❏ 1 part respect for the independence and autonomy of the other person. (Just because you're in a relationship doesn't mean the other person is your property.)
- ❏ 1 part respect for the other person's feelings.
- ❏ 1 part respect for her/his sexual desires.
- ❏ 1 part self-respect. (So you don't betray yourself, do things you'll regret, or get walked all over.)

Add:
- ❏ 1 part honesty. Which means, be honest with the other person and also honest with yourself. (But do this in a way that doesn't hurt or humiliate the other.)

Carefully mix in:
- ❏ Empathy. This means feeling what the other person is feeling. How does it feel to be treated that way (by you or by someone else)?
- ❏ Communication skills. Good communication is based on empathy and honesty. It is based on having the courage and respect to be as

clear as possible. Remember you communicate not only by what you say, but what you don't say. You communicate with body language. Most of all, good communication relies on good listening.

Fold in:

❏ An awareness of your own feelings, fears, emotions, insecurities. Know thyself.

❏ A willingness to take emotional risks. (But do so carefully so one person isn't way ahead of the other.)

Leave out:

❏ Jealousy. If you feel it, deal with it: Talk to someone, scream into a pillow—just don't think it gives you the right to take it out on the other person.

❏ The stupid idea that you're incomplete if you're not with someone. (No one is your "other half." If you end up going solo, you may be unhappy for a while, but you won't die.)

❏ Generalizations in an argument. The phrase "You always do such and such" is a tipoff that you're probably making a generalization.

❏ The notion that life is a movie scene where people should have sex without condoms and, if it's between a man and a woman, birth control.

❏ Most of all, leave out emotional, physical, and sexual violence: All destroy relationships.

• GUILT •

The psychiatrist says, "But why do you feel so guilty?"

Rick answers, "It's the girls I know. Sorry, the women I know."

"What about them?"

"Like, they make me feel so guilty about everything. Like I'm being accused of rape and wife battering."

"Do you have a wife you haven't told me about?"

"No, that's the thing. I just want to shout at them, 'I don't do all those things! I've never raped anyone!'"

The psychiatrist thinks for a moment. "That does set the bar a bit low."

"What do you mean?"

"I mean, I should hope you've never committed date rape. But don't you think you still have a responsibility to speak out?"

"Why would I do that? I'm not a rapist."

"C'mon, Rick."

"You're all the same. It's like you're blaming me because women face discrimination. Or get hit on by slimy guys. Or suffer violence. But I keep telling you, I don't do those things."

"Rick, may I talk to you not as your shrink, but man to man?"

Rick waits patiently while his psychiatrist collects his thoughts.

"I don't believe that men should feel guilty for things we haven't done. That is both counterproductive and psychologically damaging."

"So—"

"Hold on a moment, please. But let's not confuse two things. We may not be responsible for perpetrating an injustice or a crime, but as good, caring, responsible human beings, we have a responsibility to challenge those guys who continue to act in sexist ways."

"Isn't that picking on guys?"

"Not at all. It recognizes that in a society where men still dominate, we still tend to set public opinion. Our ideas matter. Men look to other men to define the values of manhood."

"So I have nothing to feel guilty about."

"Not exactly. Guilt is an individual feeling of remorse for a bad thing we might have done. But it's also a feeling of shared responsibility for not doing the right thing when called upon."

"Isn't that collective guilt?"

"No, I prefer to think of it as collective love for the women in our lives."

HARASSMENT / SEXUAL HARASSMENT

Not so long ago—well, just think of an episode of *Mad Men*—sexual harassment reigned supreme and unchallenged in offices and factories. Far too many men endlessly hit on women, made inappropriate comments, told humiliating jokes, stared and touched in ways that women didn't want.

Now it's against company policy; it's often against the law. And yet, forms of sexual harassment still go on, day in and day out.

The truth is many men and some women feel confused over what is now acceptable behavior. Many men feel like they're "walking on eggshells" around women at work; they're terrified that a simple act of courtesy or a flattering compliment will get them hauled into court. "Am I allowed to tell my colleague that she's wearing a nice blouse?" asks one man. "What about holding the door for them?" asks another. "Can't I ever flirt?" asks a third.

The answer is absolutely clear: It depends. On what? On how it makes the other person feel. It depends if a reasonable person would think it is, in that instance, appropriate workplace behavior.

There's a way to make sure that a joke, an invitation, or a compliment is appropriate. Learn to notice the impact of your words and actions. See what causes someone else to feel uncomfortable. Watch for signs that you've crossed a boundary. Or ask your manager or someone in human resources what is acceptable and what is not.

Everyone at the workplace deserves to feel valued and respected, not intimidated, pressured, or harassed.

Here's a handy motto: Say and do unto women at work what you would have your male colleagues say or do unto your mother, sister, girlfriend, wife, or daughter.

The goal of sexual harassment guidelines is not to make men feel as uncomfortable as women often have, but to allow the possibility for women to feel as comfortable as men. Sexual harassment poisons that environment for everyone. Like us, women have the right to work to the best of their ability, without extraneous fears of sexual come-ons, jokes, or worse.

Concern about harassment is another example of how feminism is awfully good for men. For one thing, a lot of workplace harassment is men putting down, teasing, humiliating, and bullying other men. For another, workplaces free of harassment are better workplaces for us all.

• HEALTH •

Sometimes it pays to think about the things you take for granted. You'd assume, for example, that since females make up half the population, modern medical science would pay half its attention to health issues facing women.

Instead it took feminism to really focus concern on women's health.

For example, until recently, only male subjects were typically used in experiments. This had some horrific results: In the 1950s, a large number of babies were born with abnormally shortened limbs because their mothers had been given a sedative called thalidomide during their pregnancy, and it had never been tested on women or female animals.

Women have specific health issues that need to be addressed. A woman who's been beaten up by her husband might show up at an emergency room, yet, even now, many doctors aren't trained to ask the right questions to find out if she experienced violence as opposed to an accident. A girl who starves herself to look thin is not healthy. Young athletes and dancers who don't have their periods (or don't start puberty) because they are overexercising or overdieting are not healthy. Women in some cultures who can only eat what's left after their husband and children have eaten are not healthy women. Women who live in fear of violence can enjoy neither full mental health nor a sense of physical well-being. Women who are prescribed drugs because they're legitimately unhappy with their lives are not healthy women.

Meanwhile, in our century, the medical profession has turned pregnancy and childbirth into a medical condition. Childbirth was taken out of the hands of midwives and turned into an operation. This has saved many lives, but it has also meant that far too many women undergo cesarean sections or other forms of medical intervention than is needed. Women (often with the support of male partners) have struggled to regain control over pregnancy and childbirth through the development of new midwifery programs, support services to pregnant women, and pressure on the medical profession.

We want women we love to live long and healthy lives. Feminism is about that as much as anything else.

• HOMOPHOBIA •

What's just about the most common put-down in every single middle school, high school, or college campus in North America? "That's so gay." Supposedly, it only means it's lame, weak, stupid, or overly sensitive. It's not antigay, right?

Yeah, right.

Listen to that esteemed gender theorist, Eminem. (Note: This is Eminem in 2001, before he actually defends a gay man in a scene in his movie *8 Mile*.) Asked in an MTV interview why he constantly used the word "faggot" in every song, Eminem replied:

> *The lowest degrading thing you can say to a man when you're battling him is to call him a faggot and try to take away his manhood. Call him a sissy, call him a punk. "Faggot" to me doesn't necessarily mean gay people. "Faggot" to me just means taking away your manhood.*

So there you have it. It doesn't mean gay people; it means "taking away your manhood." Consider the terms we use to put other guys down: faggot, sissy, queer, homo, gay. And now think of some others: bitch, skirt, girl, pussy. We put men down by associating them with women or gay men. That is, we associate homosexuality and femininity.

Which is why homophobia is a feminist issue. Homophobia is usually thought of as the irrational fear and hatred of gay men and lesbians. And it is that, of course—which means it's a feminist issue because it leads to contempt and discrimination against lesbians, who are, after all, women.

But it goes much deeper. Turns out, homophobia is about the fear that a lot of men carry that they're not "real men." That might mean that some guys worry about being perceived as gay. For virtually all of us, though, it's more subtle and not even perceived as being about our sexual identity, but our whole self-identity.

And what do some men do to prove they are real men, that they're one of the boys? One of the things they do is stuff that will distance them from women, from femininity. Stuff that puts women down. Homophobia is, as a friend once put it, the hate that makes men straight.

Guys who put down women or other men because of their real or imagined sexual orientation do them—and ourselves—a great dishonor.

• HONOR KILLINGS •

How could murder ever be seen as honorable? How could something that brings shame and dishonor to families, communities, and nations be confused with honor and dignity?

It happens if we have a society where men think it is their right and their duty to control women, in particular, their sexuality.

We've had honor killings in North America, such as in the southern United States in the decades after the Civil War, where a black man could be lynched for so much as looking at a white woman. Such were obviously racist murders, but they were also based on the belief that (white) women were the property of (white) men.

We've had honor killings in Brazil and other countries when a jilted husband murders his wife and her lover. Supposedly, such was the only way to restore his honor.

We have honor killings (even if not called that) right here at home when a man murders his ex-wife or ex-girlfriend. We have them when a man kills another man to prove he isn't gay. They, too, feel they are restoring their honor.

But the honor killings that are in the news these days happen in some predominately Muslim countries. They happen when women are seen as men's property. They have happened when a young woman defies her parents and dates or marries a man of her own choosing. They have even happened when a young woman has been raped. In such cases, some fathers and brothers feel it is their right to murder this young woman who, supposedly, has brought dishonor to their family.

Such murders are illegal although, until recently, were often tolerated. Now as more and more Muslim women and men speak out, such crimes are being challenged.

Murder = Murder.

• HOUSEWORK •

Hey guys,

*Great. So we had this feminist revolution and what happens?
Now I get to clean disgusting toilets, wash crusty dishes,
fold endless laundry, and cook meals when it'd be easier to
stand in front of the refrigerator and eat dinner. And you say
we guys are supposed to be thrilled by women's equality?*

From,
Not Exactly a Fan

Here's the thing about housework. It's work, you Chowderhead! Of course it's not all fun. Why do you think women have said they don't want to be stuck doing most of it?

On the other hand, work or not, there's something about housework that's basic to being human. After all, housework is the way people take care of each other in everyday life. You're a man of action? Well, this is the action of caring for someone else and also for looking after ourselves. Even if that action sometimes sucks.

The problem has been, and still is, that women get stuck with doing much more of this. Yes, many of us work damn hard to equalize housework. But, overall, even in households where both partners work outside the home, women do the large majority of the housework. A recent study from the National Survey of Families and Households at the University of Wisconsin shows that among married couples, men do about 30 percent of the housework—14 hours of housework per

week, compared to 31 hours for their wives. (This is a significant increase from the 1970s, when men did about 10 percent, or 1990, when men did about 20 percent.)

Perhaps you'll say there are good anatomical reasons we don't do more. Why don't we bake? Imagine *it* getting caught in the oven door. And don't get us started on the dangers of vacuuming.

Then again, perhaps not. There's nothing natural about men copping out of housework. After all, many men pride themselves at being good with power tools. Except sewing machines, food processors, and vacuum cleaners. And if men are so biologically ill equipped to sew or cook, how come most of the famous surgeons and chefs are male?

So it's great news that we're seeing fantastic change, at least in

North America, parts of Europe, Australia, and among other couples here and there around the world. Until the rise of feminism, most women were convinced it was their lot in life to clean up not only after themselves but also after the men in their lives. Particularly with the rise of two-income families, the absurdity of this assumption is ever more apparent. Women working outside the home said clearly they didn't want to get stuck doing a "second shift" while their guy could relax, or play, or focus on work or studies at night and on weekends. This was just plain unfair.

It's also important for guys to learn how to do all the housekeeping jobs. After all, guys are spending more of their lives single than in the past; more men live with other men. Being able to do this stuff means we can be more independent and live better lives.

Okay, here's really why sharing housework is a great thing for men. Sure, research finds that when men do more housework, their children have higher levels of achievement in school and, as you might guess, they have happier wives.

Even more amazing, when men share housework, the men are happier and healthier. They smoke less, drink less, and do drugs less. They're more likely to go to the doctor for a routine screening and are less likely to hit the emergency room. They're less likely to see a psychiatrist or take medication for depression.

Oh, and if that isn't enough, when men share housework, they have more sex.

Yup. "Housework Makes Her Horny" was the headline in *Men's Health* magazine. Well, not when she does it. And just remember that this exciting bit of data reports what happens over a long time—not simply the one time you decide it might be worth your while to fold the laundry.

• INEQUALITY •

The World Economic Forum—hardly part of an international feminist conspiracy—produces an annual Global Gender Gap Report. It measures the gap between men and women in four areas: economic participation and opportunity, educational attainment, health and survival, and political empowerment. A score of 1 would mean full equality. The lowest possible score would be 0. Their 2010 report ranked 134 countries.

Seventy-four percent (attained by the United States and Canada) might be a reasonable grade in a university course. It's a spectacular average for a baseball or basketball team. But when you know it's a measure of how fair your country is, it really sucks. It's telling us that women have three-fourths of the work opportunities, health, political empowerment, and education that men enjoy.

We call that inequality.

You don't need a degree in women's studies to see it.

The good news is that around the world women's struggles are paying off. Although only four years apart, the 2006 and 2010 figures show improvement. That's largely because of the courage of so many women, but it's also because governments, nongovernmental organizations, businesses, unions, the media, education, and religious institutions—that is, institutions still dominated by men—are beginning to listen to women's concerns. And, most importantly, they're devoting the attention and resources needed to get something done.

MEASURING GENDER INEQUALITY

COUNTRY	2010 RANK	2010 SCORE	2006 SCORE
Iceland	1	0.850	0.781
Norway	2	0.840	0.799
Finland	3	0.826	0.796
Sweden	4	0.814	0.813
New Zealand	5	0.781	0.751
Ireland	6	0.777	0.734
Philippines	9	0.765	0.752
South Africa	12	0.754	0.713
United Kingdom	15	0.746	0.737
Sri Lanka	16	0.746	0.720
Netherlands	17	0.744	0.725
United States	19	0.741	0.704
Canada	20	0.737	0.717
Australia	23	0.721	0.717
France	46	0.703	0.652
China	61	0.688	0.656
Italy	74	0.677	0.646
Saudi Arabia	129	0.571	0.524
Yemen	134	0.461	0.460

• INTERSECTIONALITY •

This is one of those trendy buzzwords around women's studies departments. Every book in that field these days seems to offer "an intersectional approach," as if we're supposed to know what that means.

Actually, it's sort of simple. It's just a suffix added on to the word "intersection"—you know, like a street crossing. Intersections are the places where two or more elements of your experience come together.

Roads don't all run parallel; they cross each other. So, too, do our identities. We used to think of race, class, gender, ethnicity, sexuality, age, or whatever as separate facets of our identity. But let's say you are a middle-aged, black, gay man. When exactly are you gay, and when are you black, and when are you a man, and when are you middle aged? Or, even more starkly, when are you not any one of those things? When are you two of them, but not the other two? You get the idea. Race, sexuality, age, class, gender—each of these elements of our identity—intersect with the others.

This idea has become central to how young women see their world. Older feminists were criticized for generalizing from the experience of white, middle-class, heterosexual women to all women, as in Betty Friedan's claim that the feminine mystique "imprisoned" women in the home as housewives. Really? How about those working-class women, and women of color, for whom being a housewife would have been a luxury? Or the single moms who were working and taking care of families? Or lesbians, who were legally prohibited from being wives at all?

Young women of different classes, races, sexualities, regions, etc., begin with the understanding that their experience cannot be contained by the single word "woman." And when you think about it, it enables all of us, women and men, to see our identities as more varied—and therefore more interesting.

• JOBS •

MICHAELS'

BELIEVE IT OR NOT!

Weird but True!!!

This is an actual job advertisement from the 1950s. Strange as it might seem, well into the 1960s, jobs were all described as "male" or "female." You say doctor, lawyer, autoworker, judge, cop, priest, or politician and we say man. You say nurse, secretary, elementary school teacher, or housewife and we say woman. Social customs teamed up with blatant discrimination to keep women out of better-paid or more prestigious jobs.

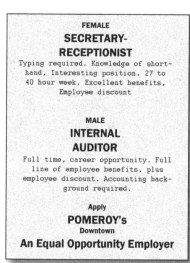

FEMALE
SECRETARY-RECEPTIONIST
Typing required. Knowledge of shorthand. Interesting position. 27 to 40 hour week. Excellent benefits, Employee discount

MALE
INTERNAL AUDITOR
Full time, career opportunity. Full line of employee benefits, plus employee discount. Accounting background required.

Apply
POMEROY's
Downtown
An Equal Opportunity Employer

Unbelievable!

DOCTOR WHO?

Here's a riddle from the early 1970s that everyone found almost impossible to figure out: A young boy is driving with his father. They have an accident, the father is killed, and the child is seriously hurt. He is rushed to the hospital and prepped for surgery. The surgeon dashes in and is about to take a scalpel to this little body but stops abruptly. The surgeon says, "I can't operate on this child! This is my own son!"

Ask a dozen people—or a hundred people—back then and they couldn't figure out how this could be possible.

We tried it recently on Zachary, a twelve-year-old boy. It took him about one second to come up with two possibilities. One (the 1970s answer that just about no one could figure out): Well, the surgeon was a woman, of course. And another: He had two gay parents.

Were people stupider in the early 1970s?

No. But our idea of appropriate jobs for women and men sure was. At the time, there were very few women doctors and even fewer women surgeons. (And, of course, few "out" gay and lesbian couples with children.)

Not Strange at All!!!

Since the late 1960s, women fought for work as a fundamental right. They knew it was both an economic necessity and important for being an autonomous person. They might want to have children, but, like men, didn't want to give up the rest of their lives.

Today, women make up half of newly graduating doctors and lawyers and an increasing percentage in other professions. Women have successfully fought to be hired in industrial plants and in the skilled trades. Women won battles to be paid equally for the work they do.

Jobs that are dominated by men still have more prestige and get paid more, even if the less prestigious are much more important. Here's an example: The time of our lives when we learn the most (by far)

and when our brains develop most rapidly is our first five years. The next most formative time is in elementary school. By the time we hit university, it's anyone's guess how much we're still taking in. So how do we reward teachers for these different age groups?

Childcare and junior kindergarten teachers (98 percent women) get paid a fraction of the salary of university professors, the majority of whom are still men. High school teachers are paid more than elementary school teachers. The upshot is that the average woman teacher in the United States earns about 56 percent earned by the average male teacher.

In the United States, women still earn about 81 cents for each dollar that men earn. In Canada, it's 79 cents. The European average is 82.4 cents.

That's up from 59 cents in the mid-1970s. But women are still bumping into prejudice. Women still hit their heads on the "glass ceiling," above which it is difficult to rise.

Meanwhile, millions of women continue to work in offices and factories poisoned by sexual harassment.

Truly True!

We guys welcome women's efforts for equality in the workplace. These days, our families need two good incomes. A diverse workplace is more responsive to a changing economic world and just more fun. Women bring diverse perspectives. And, anyway, it's our wives, sisters, mothers, daughters, and friends we're talking about here.

• JOKES •

QUESTION: *How many feminists does it take to screw in a light bulb?*

ANSWER: That's not funny.

That's the rap on feminism. No sense of humor. They get all angry at jokes about women. Why don't they just lighten up?

In the workplace, at school, or just hanging with friends, we tell jokes for a variety of reasons: To connect with others, or perhaps to feel more in control when we feel insecure or competitive, or simply because humans seem to enjoy laughing. We use humor to cut through the tension, to ease the strain, and to build camaraderie.

But who is the object of our humor? It's true, we sometimes joke about those above us on the social ladder. But as often as not, we joke about those who aren't valued as highly—people who face discrimination or who are stigmatized, such as women, gays and lesbians, and racial, ethnic, or religious minorities.

The function of this type of humor seems to be to reassure us that we're doing okay, that we're actually better than someone else. These types of jokes often reinforce prejudice, even if that isn't the intention.

Jokes don't exist in a vacuum. That's why a woman telling a joke that denigrates men doesn't usually have the same hurtful potential as a man telling a joke that denigrates women. Or a joke about straights versus a joke about gays. Or a joke that white people tell about black people versus the other way around. Or a joke that someone tells about his or her own group.

There's another issue about jokes. A joke you tell to your friends may be your business, but it's different when you tell it in public places like work or school. Different rules apply. Some jokes just aren't appropriate in these places, in part because we all deserve a place to work or study where we feel safe and respected, where we don't feel put down or threatened even if "it's only a joke." Without that safety, we can't live up to our potential and we find ourselves in a hostile working environment—a mere joke, whatever the intention of the teller, becomes a form of harassment.

Like men, women who believe in equality have just as good (or just as bad) a sense of humor. They just know that when the jokes are antiwomen, it's building on centuries of denigration—like, for example, when jokes about wife beating or rape were seen by some as funny.

We guess an entry on jokes should end with a punch line. So how about this:

QUESTION: *How many men does it take to join women in creating equality.*
ANSWER: Just watch!

• KIDS / CHILDCARE •

REPORT FROM THE SECRET SOCIETY OF THOSE MEN WHO DESIGNED WAYS TO KEEP WOMEN DOWN

"Order! Order!" called the chairman as he pounded his gavel.

An affable-looking man in a politician's suit leapt to his feet. "Mr. Chairman, we have an emergency on our hands."

Murmurs of alarm echoed off the marble walls.

An industrialist stood. "We've had the same report, too."

The chairman said, "Yes, gentlemen, we have long been afraid this moment would come. Mr. Secretary, would you please give the report from the Really-Secret Subcommittee of The Secret Society of Those Men Who Designed Ways to Keep Women Down?"

The secretary, a well-groomed man, rose. "Back in World War II, women flooded into the factories and offices. They took on all the work our men had been doing. At the end of the war, we had a problem. We didn't want an angry bunch of unemployed men on our hands. So we fired the women or simply convinced them that women actually weren't made to do the heavy, dirty jobs. Their job was to be a housewife."

A newspaperman, wearing a fedora with his press card jammed in the band, took over. "We did a damned fine job. When we wrote what a woman did, we said, 'She didn't work, she was only a housewife.' We referred to a woman by the first and last name of her husband, you know, like Mrs. Tom Perkins—as far as anyone was concerned she didn't even exist!"

A scientist stumbled to his feet, almost tripping on his lab coat. "We proved that looking after the kids was what women were designed to do."

The secretary continued: "Well, as we know, when women started getting uppity in the late 1960s and 1970s they started imagining they could do any job just as well as men. They even thought they had the right to pursue jobs and careers."

Amid great laughter at the absurdity of this, a priest stood up. "My children," he said sadly, "we did our best to convince them their place was in the home with the kids, but fewer and fewer were listening."

The politician shrugged. "I needed their votes so I said of course they were capable of doing whatever they wanted."

There were catcalls and the crowd broke into restless murmurs. The politician held up a finger and a smile crept over his face. "But how were they supposed to work outside the home if we didn't fund childcare?"

The crowd howled with laughter and applause filled the air.

The secretary said, "Sure, many working-class women had long needed to hold down an outside job, but this need for childcare was a contagion. So women started leaving their kids with neighbors or in lousy, for-profit childcare centers. This wasn't good enough for some of those rabble rousers, which led to the first calamity: Those damn feminists started demanding childcare! As part of our education system! In schools, in community centers, at the workplace!"

The industrialist said, "And just how would we pay for such extravagance? We've worked hard to make sure corporate taxes were going down. No way we'd want to pay for childcare for our workers."

The secretary said, "Yes, it was a manly effort by all of us to resist these idiotic demands, but women and some men kept starting childcare centers. They talked about high-quality, not-for-profit centers, where children were getting the attention they deserved and both parents could work without worrying about their kids. Whatever that's supposed to mean. They kept pushing and, here and there, there was some government support for childcare."

The politician said, "Well, we did need to ensure that we had a ready workforce."

The secretary said, "Some businesses even started childcare centers. They said it was good for their business, if you can believe that."

"Damn traitors," snarled the industrialist.

A man who hadn't spoken jumped up and said, "None of this is new. So what's the crisis you're talking about?"

The chairman now spoke, his face ashen, his voice trembling. "It's the men."

"What?!" shouted voices from around the room.

The chairman said, "We have conclusive reports that men are deserting us on this issue. Most men think that women have as much right to work outside the home as they do. Men say they need two family incomes. What's more, most men now want to be active fathers. And they're saying that parents, and not only women, need childcare."

The industrialist said, "Fine. We'll start a new company. 'Daycares R Us.'"

An opinion pollster jumped to his feet. "It won't fly. These people don't want their kids warehoused. They want high-quality, loving, nurturing environments for their children."

"Jesus," whispered the priest before he could stop himself.

The minister at his side said, "I think Jesus would support this one."

Cries of "Traitor!" and "Judas!" filled the room.

Here and there, several men stood up and furtively headed for the back of the room.

The chairman called to them, "You can't leave yet! We're not done."

One of the men said, "We'd like to stay, of course." He looked embarrassed. "But this is the day we all need to pick up our kids from the daycare center."

LANGUAGE / WORDS THAT MAKE WOMEN DISAPPEAR

There once was a woman named Leah. Her boss called her "my lovely assistant." Her boss was The Amazing Crisco, a famous magician (or so he said) who performed in cheesy nightclubs.

Leah had a problem.

She kept disappearing.

Not in his hackneyed tricks that were so flimsy that even an eight-year-old could see how they worked, but in the words that he used, in the words used in newspapers and textbooks, in the words on television and in religion.

At church, Leah wondered why Noah's wife didn't even rate a name.

At the museum, she wondered if there were only "ancient men" and "cavemen" or if they also had some women along.

She wondered how humans had reproduced over the eons when it was only the story of "mankind."

When she read about politics or business, she noticed that it was always a "chairman" in charge, even at the odd times when the chairman happened to have a vagina instead of a penis.

She wondered why the nice woman who delivered the mail was a postman, all evidence to the contrary.

And even when she and other women made an appearance, she

felt diminished by the words used to describe her: She was thirty years old and still got referred to as a girl. She was a strong, capable (and, yes, lovely) woman, but she got called "chick" as if she were a fluffy little plaything.

One day Leah read about an interesting study. Researchers asked some corporate hiring types how much salary they would pay a certain woman. Half of them were given a description of a thirty-five-year-old woman's training and capabilities. The other half were given the exact same description except, this time, she was referred to as a girl, not a woman. How much did they think she was worth? The hiring types who were hiring the "woman" said she was worth $10,000 more per year than the ones hiring the "girl."

Leah read this and realized that language really mattered.

She started dreaming of a world of humans and humankind, of letter carriers and committee chairs, of ancient humans, and grown women who actually were called women.

She told The Amazing Crisco that she was happy to be his assistant (at least, she thought, until she learned the tricks of the trade herself), but she refused to be described as "lovely" and insisted she be called "my most capable assistant."

After all, she was the one who knew not only how to disappear, but how to come back in her full glory.

• LISTENING •

If we men want to really understand what women's lives are all about, we've got to do some listening. (Similarly, as two guys who happen to be white, the only way we can really understand the reality of racism in the lives of black, Hispanic, indigenous, Muslim, or Asian men is to ask them about their lives and then listen to what they have to say.)

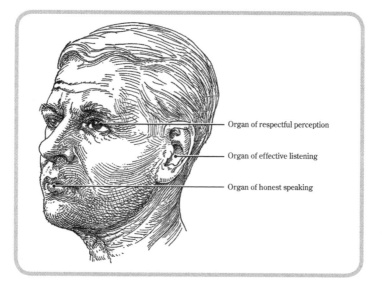

Organ of respectful perception

Organ of effective listening

Organ of honest speaking

TIPS FOR LISTENING:

❑ Try not to get defensive. Just listen.

❑ Remember that listening to women doesn't mean feeling guilty about being a man. (But it likely means you'll feel pretty pissed off at some of the things some men think and do.)

❏ Pay attention. Listening and checking email don't work well together.

❏ Listening doesn't mean you have to agree with everything you hear. It's not like women (or any other group) have a monopoly on the truth.

❏ If you don't agree, don't flip into attack mode. Wait your turn to speak. Ask some questions. Clarify. Try to understand where she's coming from. Express your own thoughts. Find common ground.

❏ Listening does not mean you have to accept abusive language, abusive behavior, or ridiculous generalizations about "all men" or "you guys." Listen with respect, but also expect respect for your own integrity and ideas.

❏ Listening means we recognize that we live in a society where certain groups still dominate the airwaves. In our culture, that means that men, white people, heterosexuals, and the middle-class and wealthy, for example, tend to control the education system, media, governments, and big religious establishments with the result that they still have a disproportionate say in defining what is real. Listening gives a chance for you to hear other voices.

Listening. Try it. You won't believe what you'll learn.

• LOVE •

NINE REASONS WHY WE KNOW THAT FEMINISTS LOVE MEN

♀♥♂ : By insisting that fathers play an equal role in raising children, feminists show great faith in our capacity as nurturers and caregivers.

♀♥♂ : Why bother campaigning to end men's violence against women if you thought that men were naturally violent—born to hit, rape, and kill? Work to end men's violence is based on an assumption about the goodness of men, that men can do better and most men do do better than that (in spite of the evidence that some of our brothers present to the contrary).

♀♥♂ : Eight thousand years of patriarchy could have convinced women's organizations not to trust men on any account. But increasingly, these days, those very organizations are reaching out to engage men in their communities.

♀♥♂ : Most feminists live with men and love men—their husbands and sons, brothers and fathers. Being independent doesn't mean not loving men! And as mothers, they want nothing less for their sons than they do for their daughters: to be safe, happy, and fulfilled.

♀♥♂ : Most feminists are heterosexual—they're actually sexually attracted to us. They love us so much they're willing to suspend everything they know about violence and assault to get in the same bed with us. (And the lesbians we know may not want to hit the hay with us, but there are a lot of people we love in life who we don't want to sleep with.)

♀♥♂ : Feminists know it's impossible for women to liberate themselves from the narrow demands of patriarchy unless men liberate themselves too. In spite of centuries of grief, they invite us to join them in healing the world. They know it's going to take both women and men to create a world of equality and gender justice.

♀♥♂ : Because they know we're not so different: We all need to feel love, to be held, to be heard, to be free.

♀♥♂ : Because they know we're so much better than how we've often learned how to act.

♀♥♂ : They continue to let us control the TV remote.

We, with love, shall force our brothers to see themselves as they are, to cease fleeing from reality and begin to change it.
—James Baldwin, *The Fire Next Time*, 1962

MACHO / MACHISMO: AN INTERVIEW WITH TWO AUTHORS

FAMOUS INTERVIEWER: Michael K-1, let's start with you. What's it like having such a big dick?

Michael K-1: Pretty awesome. Except when you're standing up in front of a group of people and it comes out the bottom of your pant leg.

Famous interviewer: Now, Michael K-2, I read in one of your autobiographies that you actually felt an emotion once.

Michael K-2: And I'm man enough to say so. Yeah. I had one of those once. It's a bitch, but I'd just had all my arms and legs slowly chewed off by this friggin' pack of wild hogs and right then the waiter comes and wants me to sign the credit card slip and I don't mind saying I was pretty pissed off at him.

Famous interviewer: Have you ever met a girl who didn't want to get it on with you that second?

Michael K-1: Tell you the truth, it did happen once. I'd just met Mother Teresa for the first time and, I mean, I got no vibes from her at all. Strange but true.

Famous interviewer: What's it like being the King of the Castle? The Boss of the Hoss?

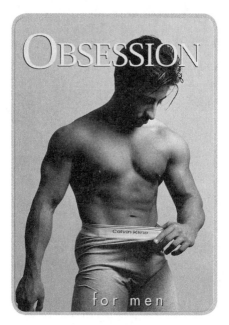

Michael K-2: I wouldn't have it any other way. I said to the wife when we first met, "To make good decisions, to be rational, to lead the way, you need balls." Not figurative ones, I mean real ones. There's something about the chemical composition of sperm that puts you in charge. Am I right? . . . I said, am I right?

Famous interviewer: Take it easy there champ. You The Man.

Michael K-1: Hey, wait a minute. I thought I was The Man.

Michael K-2: You got to be The Man last week.

Michael K-1: That's because . . .

Famous interviewer (ducking for cover): But first, this important message . . .

MADISON AVENUE / ADVERTISING

Between us guys, we're not sure what all the fuss is about. I mean, we keep hearing that women are objectified in advertising. That their bodies are used to sell cars and beer. And some feminists claim those aren't even their real bodies! You know, that photos are being totally altered in Photoshop so they fit impossible ideals of women's beauty. Yeah, right.

Look. If you can't stand the heat, get out of the kitchen. Know what we mean?

If you got the goods, you got the goods. Right?

As two men who've definitely got the goods, we say that anyone who complains about advertising images of women (or men for that matter) is simply jealous.

My name is Michael Kaufman and I approve of this unaltered magazine cover

My name is Michael Kimmel and I approve this unaltered photograph

• MALE BASHING •

"Hey, man, don't talk to me about feminism! They're all just a bunch of male bashers!"

Really?

Sure there are some women, feminists and otherwise, who "bash" men—rhetorically at least. Some are mighty pissed off. You might even say that those who have been seriously abused by men have a good reason to do so. But most women we know—most feminist women we know—don't hate men. In fact, quite the opposite. They simply don't like some of the things that some men do.

So what about "male bashing"? Well, we think it's wrong if any woman—or any man, for that matter—says "men always do" such and such or "all men are" such and such. (How many times do you hear guys say that all men are dogs? Isn't that male bashing?) We also think it's wrong if any woman doesn't take responsibility for her own actions, including sexist attitudes toward men or other women. But when they criticize the actions or beliefs of certain men, it isn't wrong; it isn't male bashing. It's challenging a system that has given one-half of human beings a set of privileges and powers the other half doesn't enjoy.

It often strikes us that some guys are the real male bashers. Many guys are too scared to express love, affection, or appreciation for another man, and would rather insult him with a put-down, even if he's their best friend. That's male bashing. Many antifeminist types believe that men are propelled by testosterone to rape, murder, and commit general mayhem. That's male bashing. Millions of boys and men get beat up or physically injured by other males each year. That's really male bashing.

So let's distinguish rhetoric from the very real bashing experienced by millions of women at the hands of some men. You want to see bashing between the sexes? Visit an emergency room or a women's shelter any day of the week.

• MARRIAGE •

JUSTICE OF THE PEACE: Do you, Alicia, know that in biblical times there wasn't a formal marriage ceremony but two people would simply make their commitment to each other?

Alicia: I didn't.

Justice of the Peace: And do you, Clifton, realize that it wasn't until 1545 that, with a few exceptions, a Christian marriage in Europe was simply a matter of mutual declaration and then hitting the sack together? Even though the church and state had been trying to get into the act for years, they weren't really part of the picture.

Clifton: I didn't.

JP: And do you, Alicia, know that in many cultures women never took their husband's name and still don't?

Alicia: Yeah, kind of.

JP: Is that yes or no?

Alicia: Uh, put me down for a yes.

JP: And, Clifton, did you know that cultures have had wildly different ideas of what marriage means? How old you should be? Whether the marriage is arranged by parents or by your own choice? Whether it must be registered with the government or not? How many wives and even husbands you could have?

Clifton (turning to Alicia): Baby, the dude's trying to trick me. Like I said, I've got eyes only for you.

JP: Alicia, do you realize that in many of the cultures that our ancestors came from, in the not-too-distant past a woman was considered the property and responsibility of her father to be "given away" to another man who would be her new master? Did you know that in England only a few decades ago you might still hear a woman referring to her husband as her master?

Alicia: Well, that really gets me.

JP: And, Clifton, did you know it is because of those types of attitudes that many early feminists objected to the institution of marriage? Who felt that neither religious nor government authorities should have the right to say whether we are married or not?

Clifton: I'm kind of getting the drift of this, so I'll go with yes.

JP: Alicia, don't you think it is critical that all humans have the same basic rights under the law: to choose if they are married or not, to have the same legal rights and responsibilities for themselves, their spouse, and their children whether their marriage is sanctioned by a government or religious authority, or whether, simply, two people choose to be married? Don't you think that anyone should decide who they are married to regardless of the sex of that other person?

Alicia: Right on.

Clifton (to Alicia): Right on? Do people still say that?

Alicia (to Clifton): Hey, I think I'm a fundamentalist. Let's ditch the JP and go back to the biblical days when we just make a vow to each other.

Clifton: And, like, I can have a bunch of wives and you're my chattel?

Alicia: Okay, skip the fundamentalist part.

JP: Hey, you two, this is my show.

Alicia and Clifton (together): Actually, it's our show.

Alicia (to Clifton): How about this? Whether we get legally married or not, let's decide that our marriage is based on full respect for our mutual independence.

Clifton: And that we commit ourselves to respectfully work through conflict and hard times.

Alicia: That we believe in the right of all people to get married regardless of whether their partner is of the same or other sex.

Clifton: And that we agree to equally share household and child rearing responsibilities.

Alicia: I do.

Clifton: I do, too.

• MEN'S RIGHTS •

The Mad Hatter perched his cup of tea on a giant toadstool and said, "Now, Alice, we need to discuss men's rights."

Alice said, "Don't you mean women's rights? Aren't women the ones who've gotten the short end of the stick?"

The Mad Hatter clicked a finger on one of his long front teeth. "Sad, so sad. You've been brainwashed like the rest of them."

"By whom?"

"Feminists, of course. You see, the tables have turned."

"Here, through the looking glass?"

"No, Alice, everywhere."

Before she could reply, the Mad Hatter put on his reasonable voice. "These days, my dear, men are the true victims of gender discrimination. All those poor men who have to pay child support when maybe they didn't even want the kid in the first place. All those millions of men who are falsely accused of rape. All those affirmative action programs where women take away our jobs. All those divorced men who don't get custody of their own flesh and blood. All those boys discriminated against at school while girls get ahead—why, at this rate there will be no males at university in ten or twenty years."

Alice started getting that strange, tumbling, disoriented feeling again. Up was down, and black was white.

"I do feel bad, sir," said Alice, "when either a man or a woman gets a raw deal when they're divorcing. That does happen. But the overwhelming majority of divorcing couples get the custody arrangements they say they want."

"Tut, tut."

"And sir," she said, "false charges of sexual assault do occur, and it

THE GUY'S GUIDE TO FEMINISM

is terrible, but they are very rare, likely only 5 percent, compared to 95 percent of reported cases (and many unreported ones) that are true."

The Mad Hatter sipped his tea.

"And sir," she said, "don't you think it's every parent's responsibility to support their children whether they have custody or not?"

The Mad Hatter studied his nails.

"And," said Alice, "what makes you think those are 'your' jobs anyway?"

The Mad Hatter smiled.

"And the education system you say discriminates against boys is exactly the same one that only boys used to succeed at. Only now, girls are also doing well while a lot of boys appear lost in a strange land of video games."

The Mad Hatter said, "Once again, you are so confused. I tell you, we need men's rights."

Alice said, "Mr. Hatter, here's a word riddle for you. It was the motto of a 19th-century pioneer of feminism, Susan B. Anthony. She said, 'Men, their rights and nothing more. Women, their rights and nothing less.'"

• MILITARY •

DRILL SERGEANT: Listen up! You're men!

Recruits: YES SIR!

Sergeant: Your job is to fight and die in wars.

Recruits: YES SIR!

Sergeant: Women's job is to stay home, take care of the kids.

Recruits (except one): YES SIR!

Sergeant: Koplansky, I didn't hear you shout, "Yes sir!"

Koplansky: NO SIR!

Sergeant (sticking his face in Koplansky's face): What's that?

Koplansky: SIR, the way I hear it, SIR, some women have always fought in wars. Sometimes, they cross-dressed to pass as men. SIR! There are stories of the bravery and heroism of women warriors—from Joan of Arc to Mulan, SIR!

Sergeant: Wormwood, women can't do what a man does.

Koplansky: Like pee standing up? SIR!

Sergeant: You know what I mean, Shitface. And even if you convinced me they could fight and serve their country, they would erode morale.

Koplansky: But that isn't so. SIR!

Sergeant: Before I have you do six thousand pushups, Scumbag, you tell me this. You saying that women should serve in the military?

Koplansky: I don't think they should any more than men should.

Sergeant: So what are you jawing on about?

Koplansky: Only that men shouldn't be telling women where and when they can do things. If women want to serve in the army, they have as much right—and as much sense of duty and honor—as any man.

Sergeant: On the deck! Show me six thousand!

Recruits: NO, SIR!

• MISOGYNY / MISANDRY •

CALL CENTER (Underpaid Male Worker): Could I speak to the man of the house?

Man of the house: Uh, like that's me.

Call center: We'd like to sell you a fantastic new word.

Man: Uh, I already own a word.

Call center: But this one is new.

Man: What sort of—

Call center: You probably own that old word, "misogyny." You know, it's a cultural ideology that asserts that women—by definition—are worthy of contempt, hatred, and discrimination.

Man: Yeah, I think we have that one. It's been around for millennia, right?

Call center: Sure has. Many societies were founded on misogynist ideas that women were not full human beings. Because of their supposedly innate inferiority, women were excluded from all the fun stuff—celebrations, rituals, sports, power, and glory—as well as a lot of the hard stuff—paid work, military service—that was then glorified as exclusively masculine.

Man: Yeah, my girlfriend told me about that. She always says, "Misogyny is the attitude, sexism its social organization." She says misogyny provides the foundation for discrimination, exclusion, and systematic devaluation. It even gets encoded in laws, in religious rites and doctrine, in every single institution from the workplace to the schoolroom, from the battlefield to the ball field.

Call center: Oh, I'm sure she does say that. They all say things like that.

Man: They? Who's they?

Call center: All those feminists. They're all paranoid male-haters.

Man: But since misogyny is irrational, the institutions built on it are unfair and unequal.

Call center: Man, I can hear that whip cracking in the background. I'm obviously just in time to save you.

Man: From what?

Call center: Whoa baby, there goes the whip again. I'm here to save you from these antimale attacks.

Man: Huh?

Call center: You're obviously the victim of "misandry."

Man: Misandry?

Call center: Yep, and for only a small down payment and installments for the rest of your life, you can own that word too!

Man: But what does it mean?

Call center: Pretty obvious, I'd say. We live in a society that hates and devalues men!

Man: We do?

Call center: *Crack* goes the whip. Everything is being done to help women get ahead at our expense.

Man: But—

Call center: Men get laughed at in TV shows, made to look like idiots.

Man: I'm not wild about that, but isn't it mainly men who write those shows?

Call center: Which tells you how far misandry has gone. It started with all feminists hating men. Now everyone is out to get us.

Man: Let me tell you another thing I've heard from my girlfriend, and don't hand me that sexist crap about being pussy whipped. Ideas like yours are part of the backlash against women's equality. They're part of the push-back by those who want to reverse the progress we've made.

Call center: But—

Man: And like other backlash ideas, it sets up a false equivalence between women's and men's experiences. Sure, there are some people who hate and devalue men. Some of those are women and some are other men. But here's the thing: Maybe some women feel that way, but they don't hold power in society, so they can't really enforce their thoughts. That's a lot different from misogyny, which underlies centuries-long forms of discrimination.

Call center: So, you don't want to buy our new word.

Man: No, but here are seven words you can have for free: Strong men aren't afraid of strong women.

• MS. •

Once upon a time, women were divided into two categories: Miss and Mrs.

"What does this mean?" asked the little girl to her father.

The father said, "Well, right now you're a Miss. But someday, when you find the right man, you will become Mrs. Isn't that nice?"

The young girl thought about this and said to her father, "Before you were Mr., what were you called?"

The father laughed and said, "Well, Mr., of course."

The little girl said, "Daddy, I haven't even taken part in my first feminist march but I can easily deconstruct those words for women and understand they are demeaning because they define us solely in relationship to men."

The father did not laugh. He did not make fun of her. And when the little girl asked that she be called Ms., he did.

Ms. Mona Lisa

Ms. Virgin Mary

NEW REPRODUCTIVE TECHNOLOGIES

This blanket term for a whole range of technologies (including fertilization of an egg outside of a woman—in vitro fertilization—as well as forms of genetic engineering) shows just how complicated feminism is.

On the one hand, many women see these new technologies as a blessing. They can overcome some forms of infertility or use a partner's sperm to get pregnant if the old-fashioned way doesn't pan out. These technologies promise to eradicate certain genetic diseases or detect severe abnormalities. They give new alternatives to gay and lesbian couples.

But with the good comes the bad.

We also share the concern of many women that these technologies are the next big step in taking pregnancy and childbirth out of a woman's hands and turning them into clinical procedures.

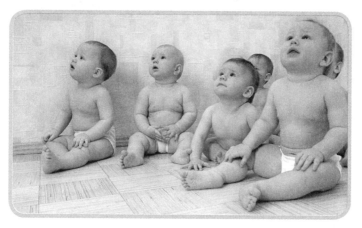

We share the concern that women are being used as guinea pigs for processes that may not work and that often involve the injection of massive doses of potentially dangerous chemicals.

We share the concern of many women that these new technological breakthroughs put additional pressure on all women to have babies—that motherhood is less a choice and more culturally "compulsory."

We too are concerned that a natural process is turned into a money-making business.

We're really angry when corporations patent human genes.

And, like many women, we worry that genetic engineering could usher in eugenics programs in which those with social power decide that some humans are less perfect than others and that we should tinker with our genes to "perfect" the human species.

· NO ·

POEM (UNDISCOVERED UNTIL NOW)

"No" sounds sweet.
Simple to tweet.
Often misunderstood
Unlike it should.

We guess some folks are really slow
The word's not hard to get, you know?
And therefore we can only guess
How some hear "no" and think it's "yes."

[Editor's note: On behalf of Seal Press, we apologize for any embarrassment our two authors are causing.]

[Authors' note: Please stop interrupting. We have some serious points going down here. . . . Damn. Now we've lost the vibe.]

Boring lecture version:

Slide one: The right to say no is a fundamental human right—especially when it comes to what happens to your body. Yet amazingly, women have not always had that right. And in some cases, they still don't.

Slide two: In many countries, women still don't have the right to say "no" to sexual advances. (In the United States, it wasn't until the 1970s that there was such a thing as a crime called marital rape. Even in the 1990s only forty-four states had made it a crime and it took until the new millennium to get a full house.)

Slide three: In many countries, women still don't have the right to say "no" to carrying a fetus they don't want—even if that pregnancy was caused by rape or incest. The right to say "no" to an unwanted pregnancy is also part of women's control over their own bodies.

Slide four: See YES.

• ORGASM •

He said, "Wow, that was amazing."

She replied, "Yeah, in a 19th-century sort of way."

Now sleepy, he muttered, "Hmm?"

She said, "Lots of cultures, including our own, didn't think that 'ladies' needed to have orgasms. They didn't even think we should enjoy sex."

"That's crazy." He yawned. "Sorry. I'm just going to close my eyes for a minute."

He had a strange dream. There were women marching on the street carrying placards and shouting slogans. The signs and their chants were identical: "We demand the right to come!"

He asked one of them what all the fuss was about. She said, "It's very simple. We have the right to sexual pleasure just as much as you."

He said, "Of course."

Another said, "Some of us prefer having orgasms with another woman."

He said, "I'm cool with that."

The first woman said, "But you see, you take orgasms for granted. If you have intercourse, you'll probably have one. We women are all different. Some of us come having intercourse, some don't. We like having our clitorises stimulated—but we all have our own way of enjoying it."

"I'm pretty talented in bed, you know."

"Do you talk?"

"What do you mean?"

"Well, how are you going to know how she gets off if you don't talk about it?"

Dear Queen Victoria,
I am soon to be married. Pray tell, please explain how I
should perform my marital duties?
—Your faithful subject.

My child,
lie back,
close your eyes,
and think
of England

"Well, that's kind of awkward, isn't it?"

"Maybe. But if you both talk about what you like and don't like, then sex is going to be better for both of you."

"Stands to reason," he said.

"So?"

"So what?"

"Wake up, you fool, and get talking."

•PATRIARCHY•

Patriarchy literally means "rule of the fathers" and comes from the Old Testament—all power was given to male elders. Today, its meaning is more general: male domination of all the major institutions of society, including government, religion, education, the economy, the military, and the media.

Anthropologists think that organized, patriarchal societies go back only eight or ten thousand years but that some forms of men's domination started long before.

There have been societies based on greater equality between women and men and many tribal societies that have worshipped female deities, where women share positions of power, or where family names are passed down through women. But as far as we know there has never been a matriarchal society with women dominating men in the way that men have dominated women.

Given the amazing progress toward greater gender equality over the past half century, does it make sense any longer to speak of patriarchy? Certainly we can point to other societies in which men's control of women remains pretty firm and overwhelming (like, for example, Saudi Arabia). But what about here? Do we still live in a patriarchal society?

Well, despite all that progress, men still control most levels of government, most corporations, most religious institutions. Men get paid more. Men wield more authority, and traditionally masculine standards are the standards against which leaders are judged. In countless studies, attributes that are commonly understood as "masculine" are associated with legitimacy, leadership, and authority. Patriarchy is as much a mind-set as it is a set of structures and institutions. And male standards both rule, and are the rule.

Patriarchy is no longer literally the rule of the fathers—some say we actually live in a "fratriarchy," the rule of the brothers. And patriarchy certainly doesn't mean that each individual man is in charge: In fact, patriarchy is a system in which only some men have power over everyone else, male and female.

Patriarchy has clearly been a bummer for women: Nobody really wants to be a second-class citizen. But in its own way, it can be pretty miserable for men. After all, the history of male-dominated societies is a history of power struggles among men, whether in individual competitions, wars, or blood feuds. And we raise boys to succeed by encouraging them to be tough, aggressive, and stoic, to try to inhabit a suit of armor that allows us to express only some things and suppress a whole lot else.

It's pretty strange—men live in a society in which we're supposed to be "in charge" but the cost is that we live shorter lives, die younger, and have to cut ourselves off from our real selves. What kind of "power" is that?

Maybe patriarchy isn't such a hot idea for men after all.

THE PERSONAL IS POLITICAL

Every so often a phrase comes along that captures an entire political philosophy. "The personal is political" is one of them. It means that politics is not just about what happens in government, but that our most personal and intimate relationships are also political. And it's in our personal life that the intricacies of male-female power relations get acted out.

Don't get us wrong. The opposite, "the political is personal," is also true. What happens in the realm of politics (for example, enacting certain policies) is experienced at the personal level.

Here's a sweet little example: Say you want to be a really involved father. The policies of your government either help or hurt your ability to do that. A country like Norway—with generous government support for both mothers and fathers to take paid leave to be with their children, with good national healthcare and good free education through university—enhance your ability to do that. A country that professes "family values" but doesn't provide any policies to help you value your family? Well, not so much. The political is personal.

The personal is also political. How you choose to act in your family, how you and your partner negotiate parental responsibilities, how you divide housework and childcare—these are certainly personal decisions. But they're "political" in the sense that they can support or challenge the existing arrangements between women and men.

You see, "political" has to do with relations of power. Not only in the corridors of governments, but in the hallways of your apartment or home. Does one person dominate discussions and decision-making? Do you have a relationship based on equality or is one person the boss? Are both persons' needs, ambitions, and desires equally addressed, or does one person take precedence?

Changing the world depends not just on voting or supporting certain government policies. It also means we've got to make changes in our own lives. It's not enough to believe in equality and then go home and expect dinner on the table and a wife or girlfriend who takes care of the children. Those personal decisions are political too.

• PMS •

We've all heard about PMS. Pre-Menstrual Syndrome. During the days before a woman's menstrual period, a rush of hormones may make her really no fun to be with—you know, moody, irritable, and liable to burst into tears or fly into an uncontrollable rage with only the slightest provocation.

PMS has even been used successfully in legal cases to exonerate a woman from guilt in a criminal trial, as if it were a form of temporary insanity. On the other hand, it's often an excuse to not take women's ideas seriously, to make them sound irrational.

But think about it a different way. Gloria Steinem once commented that during the few days before menstruation (that is, the days of PMS), a woman's estrogen level drops to its lowest point in her menstrual cycle. That is, those are the days during which, hormonally, she is most like a man.

Hmmm.

• POLITICALLY CORRECT •

"Man, you're being so PC. A guy can't be a guy anymore!"

Here we have a remarkable example of the backlash against feminism.

STRANGE BUT TRUE

The phrase "politically correct" actually started as a joke back in the 1970s among feminists and others involved in movements for social change. It was a way of poking fun at ourselves, of saying, in effect, "Yeah, let's work hard to change things, but let's not be total dicks about it."

ANATOMY OF A BACKLASH

In a remarkable turnaround, this phrase was hijacked by antifeminists. They turned it into a Trojan Horse to be used against anyone who thought that what we say and how we act might actually affect other people.

Let's say you ask others not to use racist or sexist or homophobic terms or jokes that make some people feel offended or even threatened. (Hell, such things should offend everyone!) Or you say, let's use inclusive language, like "his or her" or "humankind" instead of words that make women disappear (like "prehistoric man," as if there were only males around until someone realized the species would have a better chance of survival with some females on hand).

So you tell this to another person and what happens? You get accused of being "politically correct"—as if you're the KGB and have the power to send them to Siberia.

TURNING REALITY UPSIDE DOWN

When a person is accused of being politically correct, reality is inverted, turned upside down. Here's how it works:

As a thoughtful, caring person you know that certain language or behavior can cause hurt. So you change some of the words you use and you ask others to do the same so no one gets victimized.

What do they do? They say you're being PC. They say now they're the victims. They put you on the defensive. They deflect criticism of their behavior. They make you feel like the perpetrator of a problem and they, the real perpetrators of harm, get to play the victim. And while playing the victim, they add a nice touch: They say that feminism is all about women acting like victims.

It's enough to take your breath away.

What started as a form of lighthearted self-criticism among feminists was repackaged as a way to undermine them.

ICING ON THE CAKE

And yet more irony: There actually are those out there who want to limit women's choices and impose their own rigid moral, religious, economic, and political standards.

They're the same types that rave against those of us in the "PC Police."

WE CHOOSE PC

There's a kernel of truth here. Political correctness is, well, "correct."

It's right, fair, and honorable.

The opposite of political correctness is political "wrongness"— what is unfair, exclusive, and hurtful.

So, at the risk of sounding a bit self-righteous or overzealous or overearnest at times, we'll choose right over wrong.

And we'll do our best to laugh at ourselves when we do.

At least some of the time.

• PORN •

Fade in. Office in a Hollywood studio.

PRODUCER WITH CIGAR
I don't like it one bit.

DIRECTOR WITH BASEBALL HAT
What?

PRODUCER
Porn.

DIRECTOR
Yeah, it's pretty damn offensive.

PRODUCER
What the hell you talking about? I don't like
they're creaming off the entertainment dollars.
We're talking billions a year!

*(Stops his executive assistant, who has just dropped
a stack of reviews on his desk.)*

Hey, sweetheart—

EXECUTIVE ASSISTANT
I've told you I'm not your sweetheart.

PRODUCER
(to director)
Don't you like these frisky ones?

EXECUTIVE ASSISTANT
I'm checking the job ads this afternoon.

PRODUCER
Listen, sorry. I need to know what you think of porn.

EXECUTIVE ASSISTANT
You serious? . . . I find it indescribably degrading.
It makes us look like nothing more than playthings
of men. All those "fuck me" expressions
make me want to puke. And in case
you hadn't heard the news, our only desire in life
isn't to see men get their rocks off in our faces.

(Producer and director in stunned silence.)

PRODUCER
So that's what you feminists think about porn.

EXECUTIVE ASSISTANT
That's what I think. This isn't the Vatican, where there's
an official position.

PRODUCER
Do you hate it because you think it leads to violence?

EXECUTIVE ASSISTANT

Listen. Most women believe that porn images of
rape and violence are especially degrading to women.
Some of us think it might lead some men to fantasize
about these things. Some think it leads some men
to commit such acts. Others, like me, disagree that
fantasy usually leads to action. But I still find it
offensive and degrading.

DIRECTOR

Lots of men like it.

EXECUTIVE ASSISTANT

Lots of men like it because we live in a
bizarre culture where images of sex are everywhere,
but where we still attach shame to sex and our
bodies. Lots of men like it because they're horny and
haven't figured out how to have a healthy sexual
relationship. And some men like it because it allows
them to fantasize that men are still
in complete control of women and the world.

DIRECTOR

(to producer)
You'd be an idiot to let her quit.

EXECUTIVE ASSISTANT

And let me ask you this.

PRODUCER
Shoot.
(Turns to director.)
Get it? Shoot?

EXECUTIVE ASSISTANT
(ignoring this)
When you've ever watched porn or
looked at a porn mag, what did it lead you to do?

(Director and producer turn bright red.)

Yeah, it didn't lead to rape, it led to masturbation. You jerked
off. (More embarrassed silence.) And in spite of how vile most
porn is, that says something important about men. Most of you
guys know the difference between fantasy and reality, just like
you know the difference between a movie gunfight and real
violence on the street, between ketchup and blood.

PRODUCER
(to director)
I've got a great idea. Let's do a picture
with a porn star who stands up against it all.
Lots of tits and ass, but sort of *Norma Rae* meets
Debbie Does Dallas.

DIRECTOR
God, you're pathetic.

PRODUCER

I'm your boss.

DIRECTOR

Then listen. She's right and you're wrong. I've never had
the nerve to say this to another guy, but I think that these
porn images not only debase women but debase me as a
man. . . . I mean, I like to see naked women, I like to see
pictures of naked women, but not when they're degrading.

EXECUTIVE ASSISTANT

How does it debase you?

DIRECTOR

It makes it look like my erotic world is
oppressive and idiotic. That there is only one
standard of beauty that turns me on. That I want
women who are there only to serve me.

EXECUTIVE ASSISTANT

Ever fantasize about that, about women sexually serving you?

DIRECTOR

Yeah, of course. But that's a fantasy. . . . We're
talking about a whole industry that is based on
degrading women and telling men this is what
they should desire. We're feeding this stuff
to adolescent boys and distorting their ideas about sex.

PRODUCER

You two should get married.

EXECUTIVE ASSISTANT and DIRECTOR

(with one voice)

And you should screw off.

DIRECTOR

I want a world that encourages both women and men to
explore erotic possibilities. I want a world where pictures
of naked bodies and sex can be pleasurable, hot, funny,
and mutual. Where sex isn't about abuse.

EXECUTIVE ASSISTANT

My brother, welcome to the world of feminism.

• PRIVILEGE (A RIDDLE) •

RIDDLE: *How can something that is totally invisible be a key to men understanding what women's equality is all about?*

ANSWER: It's only invisible to you, stupid.

MORE POLITE ANSWER: We're talking about privilege. Here's the thing about privilege: When you enjoy a set of privileges you take for granted, they are invisible to you.

What sort of privileges are we talking about? Here's a sample list:

❏ Men don't usually worry about being out alone at night, or walking alone in a park, or leaving their drink unattended at a bar.

❏ Lots of guys are in relationships where a female partner does more of the housework, cooking, shopping, childcare—even when both of them have jobs outside the home.

❏ Men are still considered more rational and capable of being leaders—and if you don't believe us, see who still runs most governments and corporations (and what a great job they've done in recent years!).

❏ Many types of machinery are designed to fit the size of an average man, thus giving us an unfair advantage.

❏ Jobs dominated by men are still paid more than jobs dominated by women, even when the necessary skills are comparable.

❏ Men usually don't feel their spouse will cause them physical harm. (Please, guys, no sexist jokes here about driving with your girlfriend.)

❑ Men's activities (like sports) get far more attention than women's.

❑ In many religions, men are considered closer to God or, at least, more capable to be a religious authority.

Those are just a few of the things that most guys take for granted. Of course I can walk up to the corner at night to buy some milk. Of course I can relax in my own home without fear of getting beat up. Of course, of course.

The problem is that many women don't enjoy those same "of courses."

Which means men enjoy some privileges that women don't enjoy.

Not all men enjoy the same privileges and there are some women who enjoy certain privileges that men do not. Many things determine what privileges we enjoy: our sexual orientation, the color of our skin, our ethnicity, our socioeconomic class, our physical abilities, our religion, our native language, and so on.

We mention these invisible privileges not to make you feel guilty. (And certainly not if you're in a relationship where you work hard to make sure you have equality.) We mention them so you'll feel as angry as your sisters do. After all, shouldn't they enjoy the same basic rights and privileges as men?

• PRO-CHOICE / ABORTION •

Let's get one thing straight: Nobody wants to have an abortion. Abortion is usually a method of last resort for a woman who has become pregnant against her wishes (contraception doesn't work), against her will (rape, incest), or against her better judgment.

No one is "proabortion," as the antiabortion forces would have you believe. Just as no one is "proappendectomy." Abortion is a medical procedure performed when a woman considers it necessary. It is not frivolous: For many women, having an abortion is a difficult decision. No one thinks it's a fun way to spend an afternoon.

Feminists are no more "proabortion" than the Pope. They are, however, pro-choice. The right to choose to terminate a pregnancy is one concrete expression of the right of a woman to control her own body.

Do some women have an abortion because either they or some guy stupidly ignored contraception? Yep, it happens. But such stupidity, although not admirable, shouldn't be a lifetime sentence, turning two people into unwilling parents and creating an unwanted child.

The right to abortion as a legal medical procedure varies around the world. In the United States, since the Supreme Court's decision in *Roe v. Wade* in 1973, if a woman finds herself pregnant and doesn't want to have a child, abortion provides a safe, inexpensive, and effective method to allow her to continue with her life. Almost 88 percent of abortions in the United States (and 90 percent in Canada) are performed in the first trimester, when the fetus weighs less than one ounce. Late-term abortions in the third trimester account for only 1.5 percent of abortions in the United States (and 0.4 percent in Canada) and these are almost always to save the mother's life.

In Canada, the women's movement won partial abortion rights in 1969 and full rights in 1988.

As men, we support the right to choose because it increases the chances that we, too, will be parents by choice rather than by bad luck or stupidity. And we support it because we believe that the women we care about shouldn't be forced to have a baby they don't want. As men, we can be proud of the rich history of men supporting a woman's right to choose. (Nowhere is this more dramatic than in Canada, where Dr. Henry Morgentaler went to jail for ten months in 1975 for opening public clinics where abortions could be safely performed.)

The right to choose allows each woman to search her conscience and make the decision that is best for her. That's why feminist women support individual women who say they could never have an abortion themselves.

Imagine what your life would be like without that bodily integrity. Guys like to think that it's our body, and if you try to touch it without our consent, there will be hell to pay. Why shouldn't each woman have that same feeling of integrity—that it's her body, and no one gets to decide what happens to it?

QUOTAS, AFFIRMATIVE ACTION, REVERSE DISCRIMINATION

QUESTION: *What's the single most extensive affirmative action program in world history? (Answer coming up in a moment.)*

"I believe in equality," say many men. "But I don't believe in affirmative action because that's about having quotas."

Most of us believe in equal opportunity. But we also believe that if one person works harder than another and is more talented, that person should be better rewarded for it. Quotas seem to contradict equal opportunity, forcing companies to hire less-qualified women or minorities over more-qualified white men.

Not exactly.

Most affirmative action guidelines do not involve quotas. Rather they take into account that equal opportunity isn't enough. When it comes to the race for a job or a spot in a university, we don't all begin at the same starting line. Some of us carry extra baggage in the form of prejudices against us, where people don't see who we are but instead see a stereotype. Some of us haven't had the same opportunities to flourish. Some of us get discounted simply because we don't fit the image of who belongs in a certain job.

Some of us don't have a chance because the design of equipment or the traditional job hours were made for the other sex.

Affirmative action tries to level the playing field, to make it possible for everyone to compete equally. That does feel unfair—like playing favorites—to those of us who have always won the race.

When it comes to quotas, feminists are divided. Some say that it makes it look like women only get certain positions because the standards get lowered. Others believe that quotas are a positive way of ensuring that discrimination will not happen and that it isn't about lowering standards but examining what those standards are based on.

What quotas really mean is an institution sets a goal of a certain composition for its personnel, and then seeks to find the best people to make that profile happen. Does that sound wrong? For example, a car dealer may realize that half of its customers are now women. But the male salespeople may not be sensitive to the needs of women. (Hell, we've heard endless stories about women being completely ignored.) So the dealer says, "We need to hire staff and we're going to be biased toward women because they are the best people for what we need, even if they have less experience selling cars."

And if you've ever wondered, elite universities have long had a quota system: The band says they need a tuba player and they let in a tuba player even though there might be someone else with slightly higher marks. They have an unofficial quota to make sure they have geographic balance. And affirmative action prevails: Children of alumni have an automatic affirmative action plan, especially if their families have money and power.

Although there is much less talk now than there used to be about quotas, one place we're hearing it is in legislatures around the world. Women are woefully underrepresented. In a bid to make sure our governments represent our populations more fairly, some countries

IN REPRESENTATION, QUOTAS HELP

The percentage of women in the national legislature in countries with quotas required by law or in party rules:

Rwanda:	56%
Sweden:	46%
Angola:	42%
Netherlands:	42%
Nepal:	33%
Uganda:	32%

Where there are no quotas:

England:	21%
Canada:	19%
United States:	17%

or some political parties now mandate that a certain percentage of seats be held by women.

In representation, quotas help.

Answer to the riddle: Men have had an affirmative action program going back at least eight thousand years. Want to run a religion? A country? An army? A business? By and large, only men need apply.

•RACE AND RACISM•

Where does an entry on race and racism fit into a book about feminism? Well, right here.

It's like this. Feminism is a theory that looks at the world through women's eyes and women's experiences. It's a guide to gender equality. (If this isn't evident by the time you've reached the letter "R," you may want to return this book and try to get a refund.)

But there isn't one homogeneous group called "women." Women—ditto with men—not only come in all shapes and sizes, but have dramatically different experiences based on other central qualities of who they are.

One of those qualities has to do with the color of our skin and a few other superficial characteristics. (Other central qualities have to do with sexual orientation, physical abilities, age, socioeconomic class, religion, nationality, and so forth.)

Seems that these things matter a lot to some people who not only prefer their fellow humans to look like them, but also value similar types more highly and, hence, discriminate against those others. The larger group "women"—or, for that matter, "men"—gets sliced and diced into smaller groups that might then be pitted against each other. This is rarely in a separate-but-equal way, but usually has a noticeably unequal vibe.

Feminism is the exploration of the experiences of different women. And just as feminists speak out against sexism and discrimination against women as a group, feminists speak out against bias and discrimination against particular groups of women.

• RAPE / SEXUAL ASSAULT •

Rape is about domination. It is about having power and control over someone. Rape is always a violent crime.

From that perspective, all rapes are "real rapes" whether you know the person or not and whether you've had sex with the person before. The crime—forcing someone to do something sexual without their consent—remains the same.

And sexual assault is not only when penetration occurs, but refers to a wide range of actions in which a woman is fondled or groped, kissed or caressed, against her wishes.

Most sexual assault doesn't happen when some guy jumps out from behind a bush. It usually is when a man (rape is very rarely committed by a woman) takes sexual advantage of a girlfriend or wife, a family member or friend, or someone they have responsibility for. It happens when he plies her with drugs or alcohol to lower her resistance. It happens when he doesn't listen when she says "no."

Sexual assault is frighteningly common—study after study suggests that between one in four and one in three North American women will be sexually assaulted during her lifetime. This is a possibility that all women have to live with. That's why women (and not men) going on a first date tell a friend with whom and where they're going; that's why women (and not men) have friends watch their drinks in bars and keep an eye out for them at parties; that's why women (and not men) have to think twice about initiating any sexual behavior.

Sexual assault on a stranger is not so much about sex as it is about the need to dominate and control. It's not about horniness but about insecurity or hatred.

What about the much more common date or acquaintance rape? This may be about sex, but it's sex gone bad.

But, some will say, isn't it just a case of a woman changing her mind afterward? Of a woman who says no but really means yes? Or a guy who gets a little carried away by passion?

Feminist educators have been very clear about two things: One is that all women must learn to be clear about their signals. To say no when they mean no, and yes when they mean yes.

But feminist educators also say clearly that neither ambiguity nor horniness is a green light for a man to ignore a woman's feelings. So why is it confusing? Because to some men, sexual assault is not that distant from what we're taught to do on a date. We're supposed to be the one who makes the moves, who pushes, and who's always ready for sex. Our mission is to score.

And isn't there sometimes ambiguity or mixed feelings in a dating relationship? Of course there is. But this means simply that we've got to do what our kindergarten teacher taught us: Use your words. Figure out together what you each want to do even if it takes so long that you have the most massive case of blue balls the world has ever known.

Why do so many guys care about this issue?

First, because we know it's wrong. We know that no one should be forced to have sex against her will. It's a violation of her humanity. It outrages us to know that women we care about—our friends and classmates, sisters and mothers, wives and daughters—have to put up with this shit.

In a different way, we know that it's also a violation of our own humanity. Sexual assault brutalizes and desensitizes men (which is why conscripted child soldiers in countries such as the Congo are forced to both rape and murder as part of their indoctrination). And it casts a terrible shadow over all men, even that vast majority of men who will never commit assault.

It also screws up all our relationships. If we want a world where men don't always have to be making the moves but where women can be eager and sexually expressive, then we need a world where women don't have to carry around memories of assault or fear it could happen to them. Only when women feel truly safe, when they are certain that their "no" means no and they have full and equal control over saying "yes," can they have full access to their own desires and sexual agency.

RAPE AS A WEAPON OF WAR •

It has been with us for a long and terrible time. Soviet troops pushing the Nazis back in defeat left in their wake tens of thousands, perhaps hundreds of thousands, of Polish, Hungarian, and German women, young and old, who they had raped. Pakistani soldiers raped hundreds of thousands of Bangladeshi women during their war of liberation in 1971. Japanese soldiers raped countless women in Korea and China in World War II. Christian Serbian soldiers set up rape camps against Muslim Bosnian women in the 1990s. In this century, it is the Democratic Republic of the Congo that gives us the most egregious example: Rape and murder is systematically conducted by both rebel and government soldiers.

Why is such rape called a weapon of war? Isn't it just an extreme form of an out-of-control drunken party where some young men feel they have the right to have sex whenever and with whomever they want? Where soldiers know they are immune from consequences? Is it the outcome of the way that war strips young men of their civility and humanity? The consequence of giving one group power over life and death?

There is truth in all these things. Some rape that happens during war does happen for these despicable reasons.

But in the examples mentioned above, rape is actually used as a weapon. It's part of the arsenal deployed by an army. It is done systematically and purposefully. Why? To terrorize. To demoralize. To destroy. And to ritualistically proclaim triumph over their male enemies.

That's right. Women are being used as a tool for some men to gain points, to thump their chests, to deeply and irreparably humiliate not only women but also men.

In some cases, they think it's their right: To the victor go the spoils. But sometimes, it's not just recreation but procreation: They believe that the violent impregnation of these women will produce "their" babies, and that their triumph will be recorded genetically forever.

All of which is why as men, it is critical that we speak out to other men against such abuses.

The minister, rabbi, imam, priest, and monk were together again for their weekly coffee. It had been a week since they had discussed anger.

The minister said, "What do you think about this job we've each chosen?"

The imam said, "It's a calling."

The rabbi said, "But we did choose to answer the call."

The Hindu priest said, "And face it, it does pay the bills."

The Buddhist monk said, "That's only because you four are still attached to worldly possessions."

The minister said, "That's not what I was getting at."

The rabbi said, "What? You need a papal encyclical to say what you mean?"

The minister, a Protestant, ignored this and said, "I had a good conversation today with one of my congregants."

The imam said, "What did he say?"

The minister said, "That's the thing. It was a she."

The imam smacked his head. "My wife would kill me if she heard that blooper of mine."

The minister said, "She said that organized religions have marginalized women for the past two, three, four thousand years."

The monk said, "But I hear that in many countries women are the most active church-goers."

The rabbi said, "That's true. But face it, my brothers. Our religions haven't always been a very friendly place for women."

At that point, a young Catholic priest arrived and joined them. He ordered a cappuccino and said how much he missed the coffee in Rome. The others filled him in on their conversation and he nodded as they spoke.

The minister said, "Our holiest book claims that women ushered sin into the world."

The rabbi said, "Orthodox Jewish men still say a prayer each day thanking God they were not born a woman."

The Catholic priest said, "And we don't allow women to be priests."

The imam said, "I'm sad to say that some fellow Muslims have vile attitudes toward women," to which the others added, "You're not the only one."

The Hindu priest and the Buddhist monk looked at each other, as if sharing a thought.

"What?" said the others.

The Hindu priest said, "Your religions seem to say that men are closer to God than women."

The four monotheists looked guiltily from one to another.

The rabbi said, "That's easy for you to say, since you don't believe there is one God."

The minister said to the monk, "Get back to me when you name a woman to be the Dalai Lama."

The imam said to the Hindu priest, "And your priests used to condone women being tossed on funeral pyres with their husbands' bodies."

This grim conversation continued.

The rabbi said, "I should speak. After all, my people were the first to start a monotheistic religion." He paused. "You need to understand the times. We lived in a male-dominated society. Men ruled everywhere. And so it must have seemed natural that when we imagined God—"

The Buddhist monk interrupted with a laugh, "What! You admit you imagined God!"

"Let me put it differently," said the rabbi. "When God spoke to us, we imagined since God had so much authority and was omnipotent, God must be a male. We spoke of God as He and referred to God as our Lord and our King. We saw him as a punishing patriarchal figure."

The minister said, "We always refer to God as our heavenly Father."

The men were quiet for the longest time.

Their usual male server wasn't there that day, but as they spoke, a woman who they hadn't seen before had been cleaning off the nearby tables.

She said, "I am glad you've all been listening."

They all turned to her. The monk said, "To whom?"

She smiled brightly. "To women, of course. Many religious women believe that women should be able to serve their religion on fully equal terms with men. Most women believe that religions should not stay quiet if injustice is going on, especially if it's in the name of religion."

"Yes," said the imam, "more and more, my congregants are saying this to me."

The woman said, "Most women who believe in God believe we are equal in the eyes of God."

She paused and, one by one, gazed into their eyes.

"And, with absolute certainty, I can tell you this: Those women are right."

Startled, the six men looked at each other. And when their eyes turned back to the woman, there was no one to be seen.

• SEX •

Dear Doctors MK²,

*My girlfriend says that, like, sex is a feminist issue.
Is that true?*

*From,
Horny in Honolulu*

Dear Horny in Honolulu,

Some men think feminism is the biggest turnoff on the planet, a depressing catalog of all the things we do wrong. It's not like we get off hearing about date rape, child sexual abuse, or genital mutilation.

Some men think that feminism is a direct attack on men, which isn't exactly a recipe for one of those ten-hour boners they warn you about on TV.

But if you're horny in Honolulu or anywhere else, let us tell you that feminism has come to your rescue.

You see, before feminism, not much was expected from women when it came to sex. They weren't supposed to have orgasms. (Go back and reread ORGASM if you somehow missed that, which we doubt.) They weren't supposed to be into sex.

The women's movement put women's bodies and women's pleasure at the top of the agenda.

Back in the 1950s, when Alfred Kinsey did his pioneering study of American sexuality, he found that only 40 percent of women under age twenty-five had ever masturbated. By the mid-1990s, it was closer to 90 percent.

Back in 1975, when sociologist Lillian Rubin asked working-class women if they ever faked orgasm, about two-thirds said "sometimes." Twenty years later, when she asked another group of women, only one in ten said they ever faked it.

You might say, what a difference a few decades make.

We say, what a difference a social movement makes.

You see, it's not just that this or that particular woman declared herself a sexual being. The feminist movement changed how women saw themselves. It's about women saying "yes." (See YES.) It's about women deciding who they will have sex with: Men? Women? No one? It's for each woman to decide.

We don't know about you, but we'd rather be making love to someone who decides she's 100 percent into it, rather than someone who is doing her marital duty or faking it.

So, Horny in Honolulu, throw away your Viagra, tear up your *Playboy,* turn off that computer. Feminism has come to the rescue. And, in that spirit of inclusiveness, you can come too.

• SEXISM •

Like any other "ism," sexism is a collection of attitudes—it is a set of assumptions that one sex is superior to the other. (In that sense, it's like racism, the belief that one race is superior to another.)

In that sense, of course, there can be female sexists, just as there are black racists: All you have to do is believe that one race or sex is superior to another.

When feminists talk about sexism, they mean it as more than a bunch of attitudes. It's an ideology, a coherent and systematic organization of those assumptions. And, what's more, as an ideology it includes the ability to enforce that ideology—to pass laws that institutionalize it, create divisions to sustain it, and to create nearly insurmountable barriers. That part women cannot do (nor can black people in a white-dominated society).

As a result, eliminating sexism is not simply going to happen by getting all men (and plenty of women) into therapy to change our attitudes, as nice as that might be. It will require changing those institutions, and removing the legal barriers that express those attitudes.

There's another part to sexism: assumptions about the other sex that are based on stereotypes even if you don't believe that one sex is superior to the other. And although historically these stereotypes have targeted women, let's be clear that we're no fans of stereotypes about men—that we're naturally violent, that we only want sex, that we're incompetent when it comes to looking after babies. Of course, these sexist stereotypes are just as likely to be pushed by men as women, but all sexism sucks.

SEX TRADE / PROSTITUTION

QUESTION: *Oh, c'mon dudes. They call it "the world's oldest profession." Don't prostitutes choose to do that kind of work?*

ANSWER: Sure, women choose to go into the profession of prostitution for the convenient working hours, the integrity of the job, high social standing, the excellent health benefits, and the retirement pensions. It's often a difficult choice between prostitution and becoming an architect or a thoracic surgeon, or even finding a high-paying factory or office job.

QUESTION: *Stop being sarcastic. There are a lot of crappy jobs out there that women (and men) would rather not be doing.*

ANSWER: That's true. And that's why some women in the sex trade have defended their jobs and their right to work as a prostitute.

QUESTION: *So women should have the right to choose to be prostitutes?*

ANSWER: We need to break that down into different questions. First of all, many prostitutes don't make that choice. They're coerced into it by a boyfriend or husband. They're trafficked into prostitution—lured by fake jobs in other countries, kidnapped and held under threats to them and their families. I'm sure you'd agree that any woman, girl, or boy trafficked or coerced into prostitution didn't choose to do that. The people who traffic or coerce them deserve to be in jail. The men who buy their services are complicit. (See TRAFFICKING.)

QUESTION: Okay, we agree on that. But what about others? I saw this movie where this woman earns thousands every night and does it in great hotels with rich guys.

ANSWER: Most women are prostitutes out of harsh economic necessity. Many are supporting drug habits. Only a minuscule number are highly paid escorts.

QUESTION: Like it or not, there's a market for prostitutes.

ANSWER: The commercialization of sex depends on three related things. One is sexual repression—the fact that we're still taught that sex is shameful, even dirty, and something to be hidden. The second is that, paradoxically, we live in such a sexualized society, where images of naked bodies and sex are everywhere. Finally, it's driven by sexual inequality: Many women live in poverty and don't have options for good jobs and, meanwhile, men have more economic resources to pay for sex.

QUESTION: But—

ANSWER: And there's one other thing. A disproportionate number of women in the sex trade come from backgrounds where they've experienced physical or sexual abuse. Many young women fall into sex work because they are escaping abusive households or relationships. And one other thing—

QUESTION: You already had your "one other thing."

ANSWER:—prostitution is a very dangerous business. Many women are beaten up by johns. Women face enormous pressure not to insist that men use condoms. Many women are killed.

QUESTION: **Given all your concerns about the well-being of prostitutes, why not regulate prostitution and have government-run brothels? The women could be paid well, protected from violence from their johns, and looked after medically. They'd be well-paid government employees looking after the emotional and sexual needs of the nation. Sort of the "Piece Corps." Get it?**

ANSWER: Then we're saying that, as a society, we should be selling women's bodies. Well, we have a problem with that.

QUESTION: Isn't a model selling her body? Isn't someone who's destroying her body working in a factory or farm selling her body? Aren't you just being uptight about certain parts of her body and uptight about sex?

ANSWER: But we still have to ask ourselves, would I want my wife, or daughter, or sister, or friend to be a prostitute?

QUESTION: Then it's you who are missing the point. I'm guessing you're middle-class guys whose wives, daughters, and friends have other options.

ANSWER: You're right. Which is why a complicated issue like ending prostitution can't just be a discussion about selling sex or criminalizing the buying of sex. It's got to be part of a much bigger discussion on economic transformation and greater social equality so no one is forced to take horrible jobs. It's got to be part of a discussion about ending our ridiculous drug laws that criminalize the use of certain drugs rather than seeing addiction as a medical problem. It's about challenging racism and other forms of discrimination that erect huge barriers to certain people and foster a terrain where those women don't have other opportunities. It's about a society where women can be free to express themselves sexually, so more male-female relationships are satisfying to both sexes.

QUESTION: *So you're saying, this is one very complicated issue.*
ANSWER: That much we agree on fully!

• SEXUAL ORIENTATION •

"Hey, wait a minute. I thought you guys said this is a book about feminism and women's equality and what this means for guys. Now you're pulling a fast one, the old bait and switch."

Well, sexual orientation is a feminist issue.

For one thing, we've all heard those stereotypes of feminists. You know, lesbians who wear lumberjack shirts.

After years of careful research and reading a vast body of impenetrable scholarly articles, we've uncovered the truth about this stereotype:

It's sometimes true.

Yes, some feminists are lesbians. (Some even wear flannel shirts.)

Then again, some antifeminists are lesbians.

And most feminists (like most antifeminists) are heterosexual. (And without a flannel shirt to be seen.)

Estimates vary, but in the general population, 5 to 10 percent of women and men are more sexually interested in members of their own sex than the other.

That's cool with us and, even if it weren't, we don't think those 5 or 10 percent would give a damn. They'd say (and rightly so) that it's up to each person to love whomever they choose. And they don't even have to love 'em: It's all our right to be attracted to whomever we choose. Okay, forget the attraction. Just have sex with whomever we choose. (Uh, within reason of course. And the law. No close relatives, and no children.)

Sexual orientation has remained a women's equality issue because in most (but not all) parts of the world, women (and men) in same-sex relationships are denied the right to adopt children or even

VICTORIES FOR HUMAN RIGHTS

Same-sex marriages legalized in:

NETHERLANDS	2001
BELGIUM	2003
MASSACHUSETTS	2004
CANADA	2005
SOUTH AFRICA	2006
STATE OF MEXICO CITY	2009
NEPAL	2010
ARGENTINA	2010

MORE VICTORIES FOR HUMAN RIGHTS

LGBT Adoption (Lesbians, Gays, Bisexuals, Transgendered people win the right to adopt)

ONTARIO, CANADA	1995 (other provinces since)
ICELAND	2006
ISRAEL	2008

have custody over children upon the death of their partner, even if they helped raise the child from birth. Women (and men) are routinely prevented from getting spousal benefits or getting coverage under their spouse's medical plans if they happen to have the same sexual organs. Women (and men) are usually prevented from marrying a same-sex partner.

Being sexually interested in someone of your own sex is neither better nor worse than an erotic interest in the other sex. Whatever turns you on—as long as all sexual relations are consensual—feminism teaches both tolerance and a celebration of human diversity.

MICHAEL: I'm here today with Michael K.

Michael: Hey man, great to be on your show again.

Michael: You got pretty roughed up last week.

Michael: [Grins] Just a scratch, man, just a scratch. [Cut to slow motion of Michael K getting totally creamed so audience can be dazzled by his toughness.]

Michael: You're one tough dude.

Michael: Which is why you don't see no women playing football.

Michael: Wait a minute now, Michael. Where're you coming from, dude?

Michael: Planet Earth, man. I mean, why do men make more money playing sports than women? It's because we're more athletic.

Michael: What would you say if I told you it's because of sexism?

Michael: I'd say you're a mangina. What're you talking about? Just look at Olympic records.

Michael: A lot of that is because for most of the 20th century, women didn't have the same opportunities. They weren't encouraged to pursue sports. They didn't have as good coaching. Their schools didn't have as good programs for them. So they didn't develop.

Michael: Maybe so, but it's biology, man. Men are stronger, faster.

Michael: True, the fastest women won't ever outrun the fastest men, the strongest women won't outrow or jump as high as the strongest men. But you're missing three things. One, the fastest and most athletic women are faster and more athletic than 99.9 percent of men on the planet. Two, now that there's more support for girls' sports, the gap between men's and women's records is decreasing. Women's sports are getting more exciting all the time. And, three, you're full of crap.

Michael: Man, would you want to see your girlfriend in a jock strap?

Michael: What's that supposed to mean?

Michael: It means I'm trying to get a laugh from the audience so they don't have to listen to your argument. Anyway, everyone would prefer to watch men's sports.

Michael: I wonder if that's because we give them a lot more attention. They're the ones that get written about in papers and highlighted on TV. We know the characters and the stories. We're raised with images of the male sports hero. Men's leagues get defined as the real things. In basketball, we have the NBA and the Women's NBA, as if it's the Ladies Auxiliary. In golf the PGA and the Ladies PGA. It's pretty clear that the men's leagues are the real deal and women don't count as much.

Michael: Listen, Michael, don't get me wrong. I like seeing chicks play sports. I got a whole DVD of beach volleyball in slow motion.

Michael: [sighs]

•STALKING•

Stalking is when one person (usually a man) follows around another person (usually a woman). Stalking can include snooping around their home, car, neighborhood, school, workplace, or even cyber-stalking their Internet life. It's often a former husband or boyfriend who can't deal with his feelings about a separation and either wants to harass his former partner or mistakenly believes he will somehow win her back through his presence.

Stalking has been glamorized in movies where a guy is obsessed with a woman and showers her with attention until she finally realizes that he's the perfect man for her.

In reality, it's a really creepy thing to do.

This guy shows no respect for that woman. He shows no respect for himself.

Although stalkers say they do it because they feel so helpless that they have to resort to those desperate measures, it's also because they

feel entitled to, as if the woman is "his," and he has the right to know every little thing she does.

It's also against the law.

So, if you know someone who's stalking someone, think of him as your brother. And, as brothers should do, let him know what he's doing isn't cool. Encourage him to find someone he can talk to. Just not the person he's stalking.

• TAKE BACK THE NIGHT •

Once a year on many campuses and in many communities, a chant fills the air: "Women Unite! Take Back the Night!"

It's a night when women take to the streets and say, simply, "We have a right to be out, day or night, without fear, and without having men along."

More and more men are supporting these nights: After all, we find it appalling that the women we care about don't feel safe wherever they want to go.

Few men routinely feel scared walking back to their place from the campus library or in a parking lot. Few guys make decisions on going out based on whether they'll have to drive alone or walk alone. Few men get blamed for getting attacked—as in, "Well, you were carrying a wallet so you were asking to be mugged"—the way that women get blamed for harassment or even rape.

The interesting thing, of course, is that in cases where men do feel afraid in public it's because we're afraid the same thing as women: that

↑ THE GUY'S GUIDE TO FEMINISM

is, men. But while we just have to act cool about the threat, women have been courageous enough to say they are tired of being afraid and just plain furious that they are afraid.

In some places, men are invited to take part in Take Back the Night marches. (Although when we do, we try to be there as supporters. After all, women are saying they don't need escorts!) In other places, guys are asked to cheer from the sidelines, or provide childcare for marchers, or hold their own events.

Either way, it's cool with us. And even if it weren't, who cares: Women are also saying they don't need our permission to be out, let alone to speak out.

• TITLE IX •

Title IX is simple. It's part of a series of educational amendments to the original Civil Rights Act that were enacted in 1972. These amendments addressed continuing inequalities in educational opportunities. Title IX reads:

> *No person in the United States shall, on the basis of sex, be excluded from participation in, be denied the benefits of, or be subjected to discrimination under any education program or activity receiving Federal financial assistance.*

As you can see, it actually never mentions sports. What it does say is that any educational institution that receives federal funds has to be sure that it provides equivalent benefits to both sexes. But it immediately became associated with the astonishingly disproportionate spending on men's and women's sports. This was one of those cases where dramatic inequality felt "normal," and efforts to redress the inequality felt to some like actually initiating inequality against men.

Schools can show they're following the law in one of three ways: (1) provide athletic opportunities that are largely proportionate to student enrollment; (2) show the continued expansion of opportunities for the underrepresented sex; (3) provide full accommodation of the interests and abilities of the underrepresented sex.

Note that this actually doesn't say "women" either. At Vassar, and other formerly all-female schools, it meant the accommodation to men's needs.

Has Title IX been successful? Oh, yes. It is, perhaps, the single greatest change in high schools in the country. Within the first six years of its enactment in 1972, the percentage of high school girls playing team sports jumped from 4 percent to 25 percent. Today it stands at 36 percent—an increase of 900 percent. (At the collegiate level, it's increased 450 percent.) Oh, by the way, guys' participation increased during that same time.

This is great news for guys. Not because, as some high schools and colleges have claimed, they've been forced to cut men's sports to achieve anything resembling equality. For one thing, Title IX has a loophole the size of a Green Bay Packer lineman that gives football a free pass from the rules and, after all, it's football that soaks up the lion's share of every athletic program's budget. So if you're worried that Title IX means cuts in guys' sports, consider this remedy: NFL teams suit up 45 players for game day (their practice roster lists 53). The average NCAA Division I team suits up about 125 players and maxes out its scholarships at 85. If universities trimmed the number of athletic scholarships to achieve a number that the professional teams find perfectly adequate, they'd save 40 scholarships—enough to ensure that no men's programs are ever cut. It's not the women's programs that soak up the resources, actually, it's one men's program: football.

No, this is great news for guys because women's athletic participation makes women feel stronger, fitter, healthier, and happier (just as it does for men). And happier, healthier, and fitter women are, without question, far more fun to be around.

•TRAFFICKING•

There might be a debate on prostitution. But when it comes to trafficking the issue is open and shut.

Each and every year, hundreds of thousands of women (and sometimes children) are lured, or kidnapped, or forced into sexual slavery.

Women in hard economic circumstances, runaway teens, and refugees are particularly vulnerable.

Some are lured to a city or to another country by the promise of a legitimate job only to be locked up, gang raped, have their family back home threatened, and, finally, terrified into sexual slavery.

They're the sex workers in brothels all around the world.

They deserve our support as men to get them out of this bondage.

• UNDERCLASS / POVERTY •

Over one-half of the people on welfare in the United States are young, white, and female. Two-thirds of people who live below the poverty line are women and children. Nearly two out of five (39 percent) of all female-headed single-family households are below the poverty line (compared with 24 percent of male-headed households). Employed women make about two-thirds of what men make in the same position. In Canada, because of a greater social security net, the gap isn't as great, and yet the picture is still grim. Eight percent of senior women are low income (compared to 4 percent of senior men). Twenty-nine percent of women living on their own are low income (compared to 25 percent of men).

Around the world, poverty often has a woman's face.

Economists and social scientists speak about the "feminization of poverty." Hey, why don't they talk about "the masculinization of wealth"? (See PRIVILEGE, invisibility of.)

• UNIONS •

ANCIENT EGYPT:

(Rough Translation: You're slaves, dammit! Stop talking about forming a union!)

YE OLDE DAYS . . .
Guilds exclude women.
End of that story.

EARLY 20TH CENTURY . . .
WOMEN: We want access to skilled jobs!
MALE-DOMINATED CRAFT UNIONS: Like hell you do.
We'll team up with employers to keep you out.

1912 WOMEN TEXTILE WORKERS, LAWRENCE, MASSACHUSETTS:
"We're on strike!"
"What for? For bread and roses!"
"What's that? We want jobs and decent wages, but also a higher quality of life in a better environment."

A WOMAN'S PLACE IS IN HER UNION

ROSIE the RIVETER

— www.rosietheriveter.com

WOMEN NOW – WE DESERVE AND EXPECT:

Equal pay for equal work! (Same wages as men for performing the same or comparable work.)

Access to nontraditional jobs!

Paid leaves to take care of family responsibilities, including for pregnancy and the first months of children's lives, or for care of aging parents!

More flexible work arrangements, including flextime and doing some work from home!

1970s and to this day . . .

WOMEN UNIONISTS: We expect our union brothers to make sure our bosses take a tough stand on workplace harassment, whether from coworkers or supervisors.

MALE UNIONIST: Wait a minute. You're pitting the women against the men.

WOMEN UNIONIST: No we're not! Anything that divides workers against each other weakens the power of us all. Remember our most basic principle: An injury to one is an injury to all.

MALE UNIONISTS (LITTLE BY LITTLE): Sisters, we're on your side.

RESULTS!

❏ The percentage of union members and union leaders who are women has steadily increased.

❏ Unions were critical in struggles for equal pay, parental leave, and legislation on workplace harassment that benefit us all.

❏ Many of the basic rights women now enjoy didn't come out of the blue: They came from the organizing and hard-fought struggles of women.

And . . . more and more, men in offices and factories have joined women in speaking out for equal pay, better working conditions, parental leave, flexible work arrangements, and an end to all forms of harassment.

• VAGINAS / VULVAS •

Dear Doctors MK²,

I'm kind of embarrassed to ask you this. I heard that, you know, down there, you're supposed to refer to it as a woman's vagina. But my girlfriend said that's only the inside stuff. She told me the outside parts are called something else, but I've forgotten and am too embarrassed to ask again. So I just call the whole thing . . . well, that's kind of embarrassing too. Please help me out.

Yours,
Anatomically Confused

Dear Anatomically Confused,

We suppose that when you say "down there" you're not referring to women in Australia.

Okay, here's a quick bit of biology.

A vagina is on the inside—it's the passageway up to the cervix and uterus. It's the part if you're a heterosexual kind of guy that feels pretty awesome to have your penis frolicking inside.

A vulva is the general term for what lies outside: a woman's clitoris (where lots of intense feelings are to be felt if you or she does the job right), the labia or lips (which come in an amazing selection of sizes, shapes, and, up to a point, colors), and the opening itself.

In general, unless you're a doctor, when you're having a nice look, you're checking out her vulva and only the opening of her vagina.

You didn't ask, but we're sure you're also dying to know where this fits into feminism. Before feminism, women were taught that their genitals were shameful. Not to be looked at or enjoyed. That's why women, too, might be confused about the names and why some of them will talk about "down there."

It's also why a brave woman named Eve Ensler wrote *The Vagina Monologues,* which has been performed all over the world.

Among many other things, feminism is a celebration of women's bodies, of which, we do agree, vulvas and vaginas are an awfully nice part.

Yours,
Doctors MK[2]

VIOLENCE: FOUR REASONS WHY IT'S AN ISSUE FOR GOOD MEN

The majority of men don't use violence in their relationships with women. But there are at least four good reasons why we should care:

1. It can happen to the women we love. Our wives, girlfriends, mothers, daughters, sisters, workmates, and friends are the victims of violence, or they live in fear that it could happen to them. We want to make sure their lives are free of this fear.

2. Men look to other guys to define what it means to be a man. So even if we're the most loving, respectful guy on the planet, if we don't speak out to end the violence against women that occurs around us, guys will assume we think it's okay. Some of our friends, our sons, our brothers, our fathers, and our neighbors might assume it's their right to use violence and assume that other men agree.

3. Violence out there has a way of poisoning even the most loving relationship between women and men. It's hard to put your finger on this, but if a woman has experienced violence in the past (and over one-quarter have), or if they're experiencing harassment at work or

school, or if they have to lead a cautious life out in the world in fear of violence, it creeps into your good relationships too. It's like the way you feel if you get a stone caught in the groove of your running shoe. It doesn't actually hurt, but you sure know it's there.

4. This violence makes women suspicious of all men. For example, it's nighttime and you're walking down a deserted street. A woman is walking toward you. She crosses to the other side so she won't pass you. You want to say: "But I'm not like that! I'd never do you harm!" What we should also say is this: "Man, am I pissed off that the actions of some men tarnish how women see me."

WAVE! (CATCHING THE THREE WAVES OF FEMINISM)

CHAPTER ONE

There was this surfer lady back in the early 1800s who lived in Manchester, England.

Actually, she wasn't a surfer lady. She wanted to be, but she wasn't allowed to. For one thing, she needed her husband's permission to travel. She wasn't permitted to have her own bank account, so she couldn't just withdraw the money. And anyway, surfing hadn't been invented, although she really thought it should be.

It wasn't only surfing she wasn't allowed to do. She didn't have the right to vote. And the laws were clear: Her husband could and should make decisions on her behalf.

All this upset her, but she felt very much alone. That is, until the day when she read this new book by Mary Wollstonecraft called *A Vindication of the Rights of Woman*.

In the days ahead she heard about something called the women's movement. She imagined what it would be like not only to surf, but to speak in public, own property in her own name, and win the right to vote. She knew that women wouldn't be handed this and other rights but would need to organize to wrench them from the men who stood in their way.

She was old when women won the right to vote first in New Zealand (1893), and she was over one hundred years old when she got to vote for the first time in 1918.

At the time, it wasn't yet called a wave, but, in effect, she had caught the First Wave of feminism.

CHAPTER TWO

There was a surfer babe who lived in southern California in the late 1960s.

Well, actually, she wasn't a surfer babe. She wanted to surf, but the guys she knew made fun of her and said the sport was too difficult for girls. They expected her to watch them in admiration and tell them how cute they were. She was supposed to be pleased when men stared down her bathing suit top.

One day, she was talking to some other women her age and they started a consciousness-raising group. They met each week to talk about their lives and their aspirations. She said how she wanted to be a surfer babe and another woman said, ''That's cool you want to surf, but you're not anyone's babe.''

And so, she caught the Second Wave of feminism.

Like many women around her, she valued her autonomy and independence—she didn't need the permission of any man to make changes; in fact, men often seemed pretty irrelevant to what she was up to. She joined a women's collective that provided counseling services to women who'd experienced violence. Her friends went to work debunking media images of women, pushing for the right to abortion, setting up women's studies programs, advocating equal pay for equal work, establishing a presence as women in political parties and trade unions, and so much more.

She caught the Second Wave of feminism like you wouldn't believe.

CHAPTER THREE

There was a surfer (who happened to be a woman) who lived in Australia. Like her friends, she had never known another reality than one where women were considered equals even though she knew the reality was often otherwise. Some of her friends weren't even convinced they had to call themselves feminists.

She never felt she had to prove that women belonged in the waves. Of course women could, should, and do surf!

And she figured that the men who hung out on the beach had their own challenges and struggles, although those certainly weren't excuses for their acting like jerks.

One day, an Aborigine woman approached her. The woman said not all women had the same opportunities. She (the surfer) might take her rights for granted, but it wasn't the same for all women.

So the surfer became concerned that all women didn't have the same chance to be surfers. She developed a keen nose for the way that women's experiences were very different based on their sexual orientation and economic class, their age, their race, and many other things.

There was a lot still going on almost two hundred years after women first started talking about emancipation.

She figured she was one lucky woman. Huge victories had been won, but big struggles still lay ahead as she caught the Third Wave of feminism.

And, girl, could she ever surf!

A SHORT HISTORY OF WOMEN'S RIGHTS

622 CE: Arabia: Constitution of Medina, based on Muhammad's teachings, gives women greater rights than in medieval Europe.

1790: France: Equal inheritance rights (later abolished).

1833: United States: First coeducational university, Oberlin, established.

1838: Pitcairn Islands: Women get right to vote (suffrage).

1839: Great Britain: Mothers allowed to be guardians of their own children after divorce.

1842: Sweden: Compulsory elementary school for boys and girls.

1848: United States: Seneca Falls conference starts women's suffrage movement.

1854: Norway: Equal inheritance rights.

1857: Denmark: Unmarried women no longer minors under the law.

1872: United Kingdom: Women's suffrage movement begins.

1893: New Zealand: Women's suffrage won.

1902: China: Foot binding abolished.

1917: Canada: Women's suffrage won.

1918: United Kingdom: Women's suffrage won.

1920: United States: Women's suffrage won.

1929: Canada: Women win right to be declared "persons" under the law.

1947: Sweden: Equal pay for both sexes.

1949: France: Simone de Beauvoir publishes groundbreaking book *The Second Sex.*

1967: United Kingdom: Abortion legalized.

1971: Switzerland: Women's suffrage.

1971: United States: *Ms.* magazine founded.

1973: United States: Abortion legalized.

1988: Canada: Abortion legalized.

1993: United States: Marital rape finally illegal in all U.S. states.

1994: Great Britain: Marital rape made illegal.

2006: United Arab Emirates: Women's suffrage won.

WHITE RIBBON CAMPAIGN

On December 6, 1989, a man marched into a lecture hall at the University of Montreal and murdered fourteen women whom he blamed for his own failure to get into engineering school. It was a crime almost unheard of in Canada and instantly sparked a national discussion on violence against women that gripped the media, classrooms, places of worship, union halls, offices, and governments.

Namibia WRC

Two years later, three men were challenged by the women in their lives to do something to reach men. With no resources, they started the White Ribbon Campaign (WRC). It quickly spread across Canada and, since then, to more than sixty countries, making it the world's largest effort of men working to end men's violence against women.

White Ribbon is an educational campaign. The WRC encourages men and boys to examine their own attitudes and behavior and to

Guatemala WRC   **Cambodia WRC**

learn to challenge sexism and violence around them. The ribbon is a public promise not to commit, condone, or remain silent about violence against women.

The WRC is politically nonpartisan and reaches out to men right across the political and social spectrum. And it's a totally decentralized campaign: No one owns it, no one controls it. Its character and focus is shaped by the needs and ideas of each community.

Its rapid spread around the world happened because of the impact and inspiration of courageous women, but also because there are a lot of good men out there who want to make a difference.

Check out www.whiteribbon.com or the WRC in your own country or community.

WOMEN'S SHELTERS AND CRISIS CENTERS

You've probably got one, maybe many, in your community, but you may not even know it. Shelters are a place for women escaping abusive relationships, sometimes fleeing with little more than the shirts on their backs, often with their children in tow. Crisis centers are places for women who have been sexually assaulted or simply need someone to talk to.

The network of shelters and crisis centers across the country and around the world didn't come into being because governments realized that women were desperate for these services. They started because there was a women's movement in the 1970s that knew it not only had to push for changes in attitudes and laws, but also to offer these desperately needed services. Only now that they've gotten established, do many get at least some financial support from different levels of government.

These were, and still are, brave women who work in these shelters. They usually don't get written about in newspapers or shown on TV. But they're genuine heroes. As women we care about, they deserve our thanks.

Here are some other men who should be saying thanks: There's good evidence that shelters are saving the lives not only of women but also of men. In the United States, for example, in 1976, 1,596 women and 1,348 men were murdered by their spouse or partner; thirty years later, in 2006, the number had fallen to 1,159 women and only 385 men. When men are killed by women, those women are usually acting in self-defense or because they feel so totally trapped and as desperate as a prisoner of war that they sadly think that murder is their only way out. Once women have a way out, men's lives are saved.

And the women bashers out there say that feminism is antimale!

•WOMEN'S STUDIES•

WS 101 (Tuesday/Thursday). Why, you ask, should you take this course? You're a man, after all. Then again, people take botany and they're not plants. And what about "men's studies"?

The first women's studies courses started in the late 1960s and early 1970s for two simple reasons:

1. women were woefully underrepresented in the academic world;
2. women's experiences were almost absent in academia. It was hard to find women writers in English courses, unusual to hear about women scientists in science courses, and history focused pretty much on the exploits of famous men (in particular, famous men of the wealthy, white persuasion).

So, some pretty courageous women decided to take on the academic establishment and build courses around the experiences and insights of women.

Over time, some of these programs came to be called women's and gender studies, in part because they were also studying men and masculinity and people of diverse gender orientations.

And what about men's studies? Over the past couple of decades, we've seen the emergence of a new field, what you can think of as critical studies of men and our many different expressions of masculinity. Not just treating men as the embodiment of humanity, but as worth studying *as men.*

So, guys, you don't have to feel left out.

But you may want to check out the world from the vantage point of women. It's pretty amazing what we left out.

• XX / XY •

So, this XY chromosome pair sidles up to a pretty-looking XX at a bar. "Hey hot stuff," he says, "How about your type hooking up with my type?"

She replies, "And what type is that?"

"You know, sweet pea, I'm from Mars and you're from Venus."

She looks at him blankly.

Undeterred, he says, "You know, me man, you woman. Different planets. Right?"

"You tell me. I'm just a dumb XX."

The XY tips back his hat and looks her up and down. "Well, the way I see it, you and me are different. Head to tail, top to bottom. Different bodies, different brains, different behavior. All because I'm an XY and you girls are double Xs."

The XX sips her drink slowly as if trying to decide what to say. Finally, she replies. "You know, for centuries, men said that because of our biological differences, we shouldn't be allowed to do one thing or another. Some said we were too fragile. Some said getting an education or doing certain jobs or being assertive just didn't fit in with being a double-X."

The XY throws up his hands to stop her. "That ain't me, babe. I think women are every bit as smart and capable."

"So?"

"Just that we're different. Speak different languages, hear things differently. Hey, in some ways you're better—you even got that better connection between the two sides of your brain, you know, that corpus thing . . . "

"Corpus callosum. And it turned out that research was bogus

even though people still refer to it to prove that our brains are supposedly different."

"Anyhows, we're different."

The XX sighs. "Look, I'm sure you mean well."

He nods eagerly.

"But I gotta break it to you. The research that says we're completely and categorically different is all pretty silly. One psychologist has pored through every single study, thousands and thousands of them, on biologically based differences in traits or behavior. She found that in 95 percent of cases, women and men are more similar than different."

"See? There are differences."

"Yes, but there are far more similarities."

"So you think our brains aren't different?"

"You're confusing two things: nature and brain structure. You see, our brains are always changing. That's what happens when we learn and when we experience different things. It rewires our brains. If we raise girls and boys differently, give them different opportunities, present them with different role models, encourage them to play different games, of course it will affect their brains."

"You're saying . . . ?"

"I'm saying that our society shapes our brains. Here's an example. You've heard that boys are better at math, right?"

"Everyone knows that. It's hardwired."

"Well, actually, in countries where women are close to equal to men they're actually better at math than boys. Where it's more unequal, boys are better. And, anyway, girls in Japan are better at math than boys in the United States. That's just one example of how some of the differences we assume are biological are actually about how we're treated."

WHAT ABOUT VIOLENCE AND TESTOSTERONE?

So, the XY says, "Yeah, but what about violence?"

The XX replies, "Well, that is the one area where there's a consistent difference."

"Gotcha. Males are more violent than females."

"Only on average. It's not an absolute difference, like having a penis or a vagina."

"Yeah, but it's a testosterone thing, right? That's what causes aggression."

"I hate to say it, but even that is more complicated. First of all, XXs have testosterone—let's call it 'T' for short, okay?—only less than males have. But here's the more interesting thing: Testosterone seems both a trigger and an outcome of violence."

"Honey, I like that you're brainy, but you're kind of losing me there."

"Well, take two guys with unequal T levels (all other things being equal). The one with the higher T level will beat the other in competition. But, take two guys with equal measures of T and have them compete, and the winner's T level will go up and the loser's T will go down. That is, T level is the outcome, not the cause."

"Wow. You want another drink?"

The XX ignores this and says, "The most sensible way to approach the question of biological difference is to acknowledge that biology gives us the raw material from which we fashion our lives. Males and females share about 98.8 percent of our genes. The other 1.2 percent obviously creates some differences, but much of that is just fodder for the impact of social and cultural arrangements."

"So where does that leave us?"

"If you mean 'us' like you and me together, forget it. I'm into equality-minded XYs. But if you mean where does it leave women and men—"

Recovering quickly, the XY jumps in, "Hey, I already got a girlfriend. I meant where does it leave men and women?"

"In a good place. It means that the *real* differences are not the small, and largely insignificant, differences between females and males—"

"You're not saying mine is small, are you?"

Ignoring this, she says, "Those small differences between us aren't as great as the wide and dramatic differences *among* women and *among* men. Which gives everyone, whatever their chromosomes, far greater opportunities to be *themselves*."

• YES •

One of the remarkable things that feminism has brought to women is the flip side of the right to say no: the ability to say "yes." Thanks to feminist campaigns about sexual freedom, women now feel that they have a right to pleasure. Women have sexual agency—the right to say yes to their own desires, to seek and heed the counsel of their own sexual voices.

And when it comes to relations with men, only when a woman is certain that no means no can she truly say "yes." Only then can she ask herself, "What do I want to do with him? What do I want him to do with me?"

Actually, this makes it far simpler for guys because it takes an enormous pressure off of us to make the moves.

When a woman says yes, she is saying she wants you as much as you want her. That's something that men who love women have long dreamed about. Almost a century ago, in the last line of his great novel, *Ulysses,* James Joyce imagined hearing it this way:

> *. . . and then I asked him with my eyes to ask again yes and then*
> *he asked me would I yes to say yes my mountain flower and*
> *first I put my arms around him yes and drew him down to me*
> *so he could feel my breasts all perfume yes and his heart was*
> *going like mad and yes I said yes I will Yes.*

• ZERO (A TOP TEN)•

1. THE NUMBER of sexual assaults per year that we men think is tolerable.

2. The number of cases of wife battering that is permissible before women know that our governments, police, courts, and all of us guys have responded seriously to the problem of violence against women.

3. The acceptable number of religious denominations that prohibit women from becoming priests, ministers, rabbis, or mullahs before women know they are equally valued in the eyes of their God.

4. The number of deadbeat dads remaining before men can proudly say we live in a child-friendly society where all parents are loving and responsible.

5. The ideal difference between women's and men's salaries and rates of promotion in every workplace in the nation.

6. The ideal number of cases of discrimination against a woman or a man based on sexual orientation, skin color, physical abilities, religion, nationality, or age.

7. The number of women who die because of an illegal abortion, and the number of unwanted children.

8. The number of children (and parents!) who don't have access to high-quality, not-for-profit childcare.

9. The ideal number of men who still believe that feminism and women's equality is a threat to us.

AND . . .

10. The ideal number of men who don't know that women's equality points the way to better relationships, better sex, stronger families, peaceful communities, a more just society, and simply a damn better world.

Thanks, guys, for tuning in.
MK[2]
2011

•NOTES•

AUTONOMY

As one feminist writer put it . . . : Cheris Kramerae, *The Feminist Dictionary* (London: Pandora Press, 1986).

BEAUTY

Source of statistics: A Gustafson-Larson and R. Terry, "Weight-Related Behaviors and Concerns of Fourth Grade Children," *Journal of the American Dietetic Association* 92(7), 1992, pp. 818–822. For a summary see www.healthywithin.com/STATS.htm.

CONSENT

These four rules are from Michael Kaufman, *ManTalk: What Every Guy Oughta/Gotta Know about Good Relationships,* 2009, www.michael kaufman.com. The ideas of what constitutes consent are based on Harry Brod's lecture "The Ethics and Erotics of Sexual Consent," http://harrybrod.com/index.phpp=1_2_Sexual-Consent.

CUSTODY AND CHILD SUPPORT

Sources of statistics on child support: U.S. Census Bureau, Custodial Mothers and Fathers and Their Child Support, 2007, Issued November 2009, www.census.gov/prod/2009pubs/p60-237.pdf; U.S. Department of Health and Human Services, Office of Child Support Enforcement, FY 2009, Preliminary Report, May 2010, www.acf.hhs.gov/programs/cse/pubs/2010/reports/preliminary_report_fy2009/.

The truth is that most divorcing people get the custody arrangements they want. See: Eleanor Maccoby and Robert Mnookin, *Dividing the*

Child: Social and Legal Dilemmas of Custody (Cambridge: Harvard University Press, 1992).

DADS

Source of statistics on parenting: Ellen Galinsky, Kerstin Aumann and James T. Bond, *Times Are Changing: Gender and Generation at Work and at Home* (New York: Families and Work Institute, 2008).

Source for paid fathers' leave around the world: International Center for Research on Women and Instituto Promundo, *What Men Have to Do with It*, 2010, pp. 57–59, www.icrw.org/publications/what-men-have-do-it.

DOMESTIC VIOLENCE / WIFE ASSAULT

Sources of statistics: The California Health Interview Survey data from 2007 is nationally representative and recent. They report that 23 percent of women experience IPV at some point in their lifetime. A link to the policy brief and graphs: www.healthpolicy.ucla.edu/pubs/files /IPV_PB_031810.pdf.

The National Violence against Women Survey is also reliable. Done last in 2000, it reports that 25 percent of women experience IPV. www .ncjrs.gov/pdffiles1/nij/181867.pdf.

Statistics Canada, Family Violence in Canada: A Statistical Profile, various years.

Claudia Garcia-Moreno et al. WHO Multi-Country Study on Womens Health and Domestic Violence against Women, World Health Organization, 2005. www.who.int/gender/violence/who_multi country_study/en/.

An article debunking the myth that women's violence against men is as serious an issue as men's violence against women: Michael Kimmel, "Gender Symmetry in Domestic Violence: A Substantive and Methodological Research Review" in *Violence Against Women* 8 (11), November 2002.

For a short article exploring the causes of men's violence, see Michael Kaufman, The 7 Ps of Mens Violence, at www.michaelkaufman.com.

FUNDAMENTALISM

The author of the satirical letter to Dr. Laura is unknown. A complete version of this letter can be found at www.GuysGuidetoFeminism.com.

GENITAL CUTTING

For further information on African women's efforts to organize against genital cutting through United Nations agencies and non-governmental organizations, see their 2009 statement: Legislation to Address the Issue of Female Genital Mutilation. www.un.org/womenwatch/daw /egm/vaw_legislation_2009/Expert%20Paper%20EGMGPLHP%20 _Berhane%20Ras-Work%20revised_.pdf.

HOMOPHOBIA

Quote from Eminem in Richard Kim, "A Bad Rap," *The Nation,* March 5, 2001, p. 5.

HOUSEWORK

Source of statistics on housework: University of Wisconsin, National Survey of Families and Households, www.ssc.wisc.edu/nsfh/.

Yun-Suk Lee and Linda Waite, "Husbands and Wives Time Spent on Housework: A Comparison of Measures" in *Journal of Marriage and the Family* 67, May 2005, pp. 328–336.

INEQUALITY

Source of table: World Economic Forum, The Global Gender Gap Report, 2010, prepared by Ricardo Hausmann, Laura D. Tyson, and Saadia Zahidi (Geneva, 2010), Table 3a, pp. 8–9. Chart ranked by health and survival. www3.weforum.org/docs/WEF_GenderGap_Report_2010.pdf.

JOBS

Source of statistics on the male/female wage gap: http://economix .blogs.nytimes.com/2010/03/09/the-gender-wage-gap-around-the-world/.

LOVE

Thanks to these women, whose answers to the question "How do we know feminists love men?" have been incorporated into these nine points: Laura Asturias, Kathryn Feltey, Rachel Friendly, Ellie Hutch, Anita Mathew, Roozbeh Mircharkchian, Leona Peardon, and Marisa Wikramanayake.

PORN

Michael Kimmel, editor, *Men Confront Pornography* (New York: Crown 1991), collects the writing of a large number of men who explore many facets of the porn debate. Also see Robert Jensen's book, *Getting Off* (Brooklyn: South End Press, 2007) and Pamela Paul, *Pornified* (New York: Holt Paperbacks, 2006).

PRIVILEGE (A RIDDLE)

See Peggy McIntosh, *Unpacking the Invisible Knapsack in Privilege*, edited by Abby Ferber and Michael Kimmel (Boulder: Westview Press, 2010).

PRO-CHOICE / ABORTION

U.S. statistics from: Guttamacher Institute, Facts on Induced Abortion in the United States, January 2011.

Canadian statistics from: Abortion Rights Coalition of Canada, Position Paper #22, July 2005.

SEX

Statistics on women and masturbation: Alfred Kinsey, Wardell Pomeroy, and Charles Martin, *Sexual Behavior in the Human Female* (Philadelphia: W. B. Saunders, 1953). Edward Laumann, Robert Michael, John Gagnon, and Stuart Michaels, *The Social Organization of Sexuality* (Chicago: University of Chicago Press, 1996).

On women faking orgasm, see: Lillian Rubin, *World of Pain* (New York: Basic Books, 1975), and Lillian Rubin, *Erotic Wars* (New York: Farrar, Straus, 1993).

TITLE IX

Data on the increase in girls' and womens' participation: www.nfhs .org/Participation/HistoricalSearch.aspx.

UNDERCLASS / POVERTY

Source of U.S. Statistics: Census Bureau in the report C2. Household Relationship and Living Arrangements of Children Under 18 Years, by

Age and Sex: 2010, available at www.census.gov/population/www/socdemo/hhfam/cps2010.html.

Source of Canadian Statistics: Statistics Canada, Persons in low income after tax, 2008, www40.statcan.gc.ca/l01/cst01/famil19a-eng.htm

XX / XY

For a general debunking of the whole sex difference model: Janet Hyde, "The Gender Similarities Hypothesis," American Psychologist 60 (2005): pp. 581–592.

On women's and men's math scores: Janet Hyde, et al., "Gender Similarities Characterize Math Performance," Science 321 (July 25, 2008): pp. 494–495.

On the bogus corpus callosum research: See, for example, the popular account in Lise Eliot, Pink Brain Blue Brain (New York: Houghton Mifflin Harcourt Publishing Company, 2009), pp. 10–11.

ACKNOWLEDGMENTS

We are grateful to Chloe Angyal, Jennifer Baumgardner, Michelle Haimoff, Amanda Kennedy, Cheryl Llewellyn, Courtney Martin, Rachel Simmons, Jean-Anne Sutherland, Jessica Valenti, and Meredith Villano, for their comments on the draft of this book—and to Gary Barker, for his help with some examples—but do not hold them responsible for any errors or for our own take on the issues at hand. We are particularly grateful to Amy Aronson for her comments on earlier drafts and also for feedback and encouragement from Betty Chee, Liam Kaufman Simpkins, Lisa Alexander, Chloe Hung, and Zachary Kimmel.

Thanks to Seal Press, in particular our editors Merrik Bush-Pirkle, Brooke Warner, copy editor Nina Wegner, and designers Kate Basart and Tabitha Lahr.

We'd also like to acknowledge the many men around the world—now, far too many to name—who, for many years, have explored what feminism means for men.

• ABOUT THE AUTHORS •

MICHAEL KAUFMAN, PHD, is an educator and writer focused on engaging men and boys to promote gender equality and end violence against women. He has worked in forty-five countries, including extensively with the United Nations, as well as numerous governments and NGOs. He is the cofounder of the White Ribbon Campaign, the largest effort in the world of men working to end violence against women. He is the author or editor of six books on gender issues, democracy, and development studies, as well as an award-winning novel. His articles have been translated into fifteen languages. Married with two children, he lives in Toronto, Canada. For more information, visit www.michaelkaufman.com.

© Ali Kazimi

•ABOUT THE AUTHORS•

MICHAEL KIMMEL, PHD, is an activist, teacher, and researcher whose mission is to engage boys and men in supporting gender equality. A professor of sociology at SUNY Stony Brook, he has received several awards for his scholarship and mentoring. He is the author of many books and articles, including the bestsellers *Guyland* and *Manhood in America*. For many years, he was national spokesperson for NOMAS (National Organization for Men against Sexism). He has lectured at more than two hundred colleges and universities, and consulted internationally with corporations, governments, and NGOs. For more information, visit www.michaelkimmel.com.

© Mikael Lundgren

•CREDITS•

AUTONOMY
Illustration of apple pie © Roslen Mack/www.123rf.com

BRA BURNING
Image courtesy of Duke University Special Collections.

CONSENT
Drawings © Julian Kirk-Elleker and Michael Kaufman, from *ManTalk: What Every Guy Oughta/Gotta Know About Good Relationships, 2008.*

FEMINISM
Photo of doctor © H. Armstrong Roberts/Corbis Images

FUNDAMENTALISM
Etching by Gustave Doré (1832-1883).

GIRLS GONE WILD:
Jack and Jill published in 1804 by J. Aldis (Moorfields, England); reproduced by California Digital Library, http://www.archive.org/details/cdl.

GUILT
Photo of Sigmund Freud by Max Halberstadt/Wikimedia Commons

HOUSEWORK
Article from *Men's Health:* Copyright Rodale Inc., 2003. All rights reserved, Men's Health® is a registered trademark of Rodale Inc.

LISTENING

Drawing © Julian Kirk-Elleker and Michael Kaufman, from *ManTalk: What Every Guy Oughta/Gotta Know About Good Relationships, 2008.*

MACHO

Advertisement courtesy of Adbusters.org.

MADISON AVENUE / ADVERTISING

Michael Kaufman body photo © maxfx/www.123rf.com

Michael Kimmel body photo © Oleksandr Petrunovskyi

MARRIAGE

Illustration © Roman Dekan/www.123rf.com

MILITARY

Photo © Lance Cpl. John Kennicutt, U.S. Marine Corps

MS.

Mona Lisa by Leonardo da Vinci, photo by Au plus près des oeuvres!, Musée du Louvre/ Wikimedia Commons

Virgin Mary (Freskenzyklus im Dominikanerkloster San Marco in Florenz, Szene) by Fra Angelico, photo from The Yorck Project: 10.000 Meisterwerke der Malerei. DVD-ROM, 2002. ISBN 3936122202. Distributed by DIRECTMEDIA Publishing GmbH./Wikimedia Commons

NEW REPRODUCTIVE TECHNOLOGIES

Photo © Andrejs Pidjass/www.123rf.com

ORGASM

Photo of Queen Victoria, photographer unknown/Wikimedia Commons

RELIGION

Creation of the Sun and Moon by Michelangelo, face detail of God., 1511/Wikimedia Commons. Painting is located in the Sistine Chapel in the Vatican, Rome, Italy.

SEX

Drawing © Julian Kirk-Elleker and Michael Kaufman, from *ManTalk: What Every Guy Oughta/Gotta Know About Good Relationships, 2008.*

TAKE BACK THE NIGHT

Photo © Gopal Vijayaraghavan, http://www.flickr.com/photos/t3r min4t0r/ (Creative Commons).

UNIONS

Drawing of hieroglyphics © Pavel Konovalov/www.123rf.com

Photo of two women strikers on picket line during the "Uprising of the 20,000", garment workers strike, New York City by Bain News Service, George Grantham Bain collection/Wikimedia Commons

Badge reprinted with the permission of rosietheriverter.com.

WHITE RIBBON CAMPAIGN

White Ribbon photos courtesy of White Ribbon Campaigns in Namibia, Guatemala, and Cambodia

SELECTED TITLES FROM SEAL PRESS

For more than thirty years, Seal Press has published groundbreaking books. By women. For women.

Men and Feminism: Seal Studies, by Shira Tarrant, PhD. $14.95, 978-1-58005-258-0. Answering questions about how and why men should get behind feminism, *Men and Feminism* lays the foundation for a discussion about feminism as a human issue, not simply a women's issue.

Yes Means Yes: Visions of Female Sexual Power and A World without Rape, by Jaclyn Friedman and Jessica Valenti. $16.95, 978-1-58005-257-3. This powerful and revolutionary anthology offers a paradigm shift from the "No Means No" model, challenging men and women to truly value female sexuality and ultimately end rape.

F 'em!: Goo Goo, Gaga, and Some Thoughts on Balls, by Jennifer Baumgardner. $17.00, 978-1-58005-360-0. A collection of essays—plus interviews with well-known feminists—by *Manifesta* coauthor Jennifer Baumgardner on everything from purity balls to Lady Gaga.

What You Really Really Want: The Smart Girl's Shame-Free Guide to Sex and Safety, by Jaclyn Friedman. $17.00, 978-1-58005-344-0. An educational and interactive guide that gives young women the tools they need to decipher the modern world's confusing, hypersexualized landscape and define their own sexual identity.

The Purity Myth: How America's Obsession with Virginity Is Hurting Young Women, by Jessica Valenti. $16.95, 978-1-58005-314-3. With her usual balance of intelligence and wit, Valenti presents a powerful argument that girls and women, even in this day and age, are overly valued for their sexuality—and that this needs to stop.

He Said What?: Women Write about Moments When Everything Changed, edited by Victoria Zackheim. $16.95, 978-1-58005-336-5. Twenty-six gifted women writers share profoundly personal moments in which a man in their life said something—good or bad—that changed their lives irrevocably.

Find Seal Press Online
www.SealPress.com
www.Facebook.com/SealPress
Twitter: @SealPress